HIP
HOTELS

ORIENT

HERBERT YPMA

HIP
HOTELS

ORIENT

with 475 illustrations, 367 in colour

Thames & Hudson

introduction

The Orient is more than a destination. It is the cradle of some of the world's oldest civilizations, the *terra firma* of the globe's largest population and the spiritual base of the most numerous Buddhists, Hindus and Muslims on earth. A collection of cultures that are rich and deep and varied, the Orient is absolutely teeming with life, and it wouldn't be an exaggeration to call it the most vibrant corner of the planet.

Since ancient times, China, Siam, India, Japan and their neighbours have held sway in the Western imagination. Once impossibly far away, the countries of the Orient have long been the subject of dreams and fantasies. When the world was a far less travelled place, the Orient was synonymous with exotic destinations; all lands east of Istanbul were included, and 'Oriental' was a catchword for all things new, different, strange and exciting.

Today's Orient is a modern-minded, fast-moving, steadily emerging economic counterpart to both Europe and the United States. Yet fortunately it has retained its cultural integrity. This has a lot to do with the fact that there is now significant travel within Asia itself. Tourists are no longer limited to the odd adventurer from another continent –

the Japanese honeymoon in Bali, the residents of Bangkok regularly fly to Hong Kong and vice versa, the Vietnamese visit Siem Reap in Cambodia and the Singaporeans holiday in Malaysia. In fact, the Orient has turned out to be a dream destination for the people who live there. Although some outsiders still cling to a colonial vision of the Orient, its citizens see their own backyard differently. They are not afraid to embrace modernity. Ultimately, that's what makes the Orient of today so compelling: a passion for the new in terms of art, architecture and interiors is paired with the historic appeal of the old.

But even the most idyllic destinations are not immune from the havoc that Mother Nature can wreak. As this book was going to press, the tsunamis of late December 2004 hit Southeast Asia with devastating effect.

Yet, amazingly, and due to nothing other than pure luck, it's incredible how little the hotels featured here were affected. Perhaps it's a timely reminder of the vast options Asia has on offer – a plethora of escape destinations that combine world-renowned service with extraordinary locations. Yes, the region has been shaken, but not to the extent that it can dim the enduring attraction of the Orient.

the balé

A *balé* is a traditional Balinese structure: a house on stilts, a timber platform with an overhanging roof usually thatched in *alang alang* grass. But you will find no such structure at the Balé. The name is an abstract reference to the age-old raised shelter. In the same way, the design refers to Balinese tradition, but not obviously so.

Bali has its own form of Hinduism, Agama Tirtha, which literally means the religion of holy water; every well, waterfall and fountainhead possesses spiritual significance. Indonesian architects Anthony Liu and Ferry Ridwan took this aspect of Balinese culture to heart when they designed the Balé. There are more than seventy individual pools on this multi-terraced property, twenty-two of which are dedicated to swimming, two to bathing (in the spa) and the remaining forty-eight to ornamentation. Not bad for a hotel that only has twenty rooms. Then again, the word 'room' is hardly an adequate description. At the Balé, every guest is accommodated in their own individual pavilion, complete with a private swimming pool (which you access directly from your bathroom), an outdoor entertainment area and a sweeping view of the crescent-shaped beach of Nusa Dua below.

For the lucky few who stay here as guests, it's a magnificently luxurious experience, to be sure – one international architecture magazine described the Balé as having 'a majestic quality, like a modern Persepolis'. And yet it's hard to find someone in Bali who has a kind word to say about it. 'It's so minimal and so pale you need your sunglasses all the time,' is one comment; 'It has nothing to do with Bali,' is another; 'It looks OK now but what will happen in a few years' time?' is still another. It's clear that the place is misunderstood, but none of this general mudslinging has had any effect on occupancy: the Balé is the most booked-out hotel on the entire island. That's because consumers recognize a good deal when they see one. Privacy, luxury and modernity – the Balé has it all. What's more, aesthetically speaking, the creative team of Liu, Ridwan and Bali-based American landscape architect Karl Princic have proven that a design does not have to rely on ornamentation in order to be Balinese.

Critics of the Balé have clearly missed the point. The design, in all its monochrome, minimalist modernism, is still very much a response to the site. Unlike the lush tropical vegetation that defines most of Bali, the Bukit

Peninsula on which the hotel is situated is starker and more severe. It's also more desert-like in its dominant shades of bleached browns and sand. This rugged, neutral-toned landscape is reflected in the architects' choice of pebble-washed, sand-coloured terrazzo floors, and the retaining walls in local limestone. The idea was to emphasize the beauty of the surroundings and the view of the ocean below, rather than the local culture. Just down the road is Seminyak, the epicentre of Balinese tourism and home to some of the island's trendiest restaurants and nightclubs including Ku De Ta, which regularly features guest DJs such as Paris's legendary Claude Challe. In short, this is the most cosmopolitan part of Bali, and the Balé is its most cosmopolitan overnight address.

Interestingly, such a place would have been inconceivable even a decade ago. But the rise of inter-Asian travel has changed all that. Bali is easily accessible from Singapore, Jakarta, Bangkok, Hong Kong and even Sydney and Tokyo, and hotels such as the Balé reflect the emerging Asian taste for minimalism as opposed to the preference of Europeans and Americans for 'ethnic' decorativeness. Released from Western cultural vanities, designers in Asia are free to create, tapping into influences irrespective of origin. Liu's inspiration is typical: his designs draw from the work of Mies van der Rohe and England-based John Pawson, from the spare poetry of Japan's Tadao Ando and the pristine precision of Switzerland's Peter Zumthor.

It's doubtful that the young Asian couples who choose the Balé as their honeymoon destination give much thought to the intellectual *raison d'être* of the property's design, nor would they lose sleep over the question of whether the place is Balinese enough. For them it's a simple matter of staying at a beautiful place in a beautiful setting. And surely therein lies the new ethos of Asian design: less dependent on tradition and so-called authenticity, and more concerned with quality and modernity.

address The Balé, Jalan Raya Nusa Dua Selatan, P.O. Box 76, Nusa Dua, 80363 Bali, Indonesia

t +62 (0)361 775 111 **f** +62 (0)361 775 222 **e** bliss@thebale.com

room rates from US$480

begawan giri estate

Begawan Giri Estate is not a hotel. It's a dream. It's everything the first-time visitor wants Bali to be, and everything the person who knows the island is hoping to find. It's a mystical, spiritual, exotic, immaculate, architectural and unashamedly luxurious retreat.

Begawan Giri was never intended as a hotel. What it is today is the result of the original owners' total commitment to a property. Bradley Gardner was a British expat who had established a successful chain of fashion jewelry shops all over Asia. When he and his wife Debbie stumbled upon the Begawan Giri site in 1989 while on a mountain walk, they had a revelation – they simply understood the magic of the spot. Bit by bit they acquired small parcels of land, until eventually their acquisitions grew to an expanse of eight hectares, which encompasses a small plateau that drops away ravine-like to the Ayung River below. But it wasn't yet clear to the owners what to do with this dramatic terrain. As Bradley Gardner put it, 'It was not until some time had passed before we were sure what we wanted from the land – or, more accurately, what the land wanted from us.'

Long before they erected a building of any kind, the Gardners commenced an ambitious landscaping project. Over a period of nine years, they deployed a small army of gardeners to plant more than two-and-a-half thousand trees; carve countless terraces into the steep hillside leading down to the river; build scores of footpaths cut from blocks of black volcanic stone; excavate a series of terracotta-paved roads; and cover acre after acre with a dense, verdant carpet of alang alang grass. No detail was left unattended. Like a cleverly crafted film, the gardens of Begawan Giri reveal themselves slowly. Inspired by legendary Sri Lankan architect Geoffrey Bawa's gardens at his Lunuganga estate, the Gardners have created the same carefully cultivated sense of natural wilderness. As a guest, you make a new discovery with every excursion from your room, whether it's a discreetly placed balé, a stone wall covered in green moss, or one of several natural springs. It's a visual theatre of botanical art direction.

The Gardners' appreciation of the property was enriched by local legend. Once upon a time ordinary villagers were loath to venture into the dense, steeply declining jungle. The only people who dared to enter it were three wise men who invested the land with a powerful spiritual energy, and it became known

among the villagers as *begawan giri* or 'wise man's mountain'. Folklore aside, a plan emerged as to what to build on this magical site. The Gardners envisaged an estate, a retreat in the old-fashioned sense where you come to recover from the stress and toll of daily life, and your personal butler takes care of the day-to-day tediums of packing, unpacking, laundering, pressing and arranging flights. What's more, they wanted to build a house, or a series of houses – not a large box with a series of identical rooms.

Though the idea behind Begawan Giri was fuelled by a longing for the old-fashioned, the form this would take was anything but. Together with Malaysian architect Cheong Yew Kuan, the Gardners set out to create a dynamic Asian architecture with a strong Balinese flavour. Where a less adventurous client and architect would opt for the logical simplicity of building on the flatness of a plateau, Gardner and Cheong chose to build their first project on land a shade short of vertical. The engineering required was formidable, but the result is all drama and privacy. The structure overhangs the horseshoe-shaped gorge that defines the property, and the waterfalls below provide a soothing, permanent acoustic backdrop. What's more, its position renders it virtually invisible from the road leading through the property. This formula provided the blueprint for four more residences, which vary in style but all share in the property's extraordinary beauty as a focal point.

With time, Begawan Giri grew beyond anything the Gardners had ever imagined. Their baby was starting to demand more and more time and even more money. With two restaurants, two shops, a fully fledged spa and another seven private villas, it was clear that Begawan Giri needed more than the Gardners could give; in 2004, the property transferred into the capable hands of hotel impresario Christina Ong. Now, at last, the Gardners themselves are able to enjoy the estate, in exactly the way they intended their guests to.

---

address Begawan Giri Estate, P.O. Box 54, Ubud, 80571 Bali, Indonesia

t +62 (0)361 978 888   **f** +62 (0)361 978 889   **e** res.begawan@begawangiri.como.bz

room rates from US$495

uma ubud

Bali is a unique part of Indonesia, both geographically and spiritually. It's a place blessed with volcanic mountains, lush tropical forests and plenty of sandy beaches, and it's also the only Hindu island in the world's most populous Islamic nation. Hinduism first travelled to Bali more than five centuries ago and its presence was later bolstered by the arrival of Hindu brahmans fleeing the increasingly dominant Muslim majority elsewhere in the Indonesian archipelago. During colonial times, the Dutch were eager to preserve Bali's gentle personality, and forbade the imams of neighbouring Lombok, Sumbawa and Java to travel there. Thus the Hindu way of life was both protected and preserved.

The island's spirituality has developed into a uniquely Balinese brand of Hinduism: life is seen as a battle between the demon forces that dwell in the sea and the gods who live in the mountains. Bali's spirituality is a big part of its attraction – the way people live and pray is linked with an extraordinary aesthetic sensibility. The Balinese are fastidious about their temples, shrines and appearances (what they wear to temples is elaborately decorative and colour-coded). Every shrine,

no matter how small, benefits from intense personal attention: all statues are ritually presented with food, clothing and song.

Spirituality in Bali is a lifestyle, and one that is grounded in the Balinese village. The more cohesive the village, the more closely its people follow tradition in terms of festivals and rituals. That's why in places such as Semin Yak, long popular with expats, Hindu customs, prayer and temple activity have declined. In Ubud, however, the people still feel a strong sense of community and have thus retained the emotively colourful spectacle of the Balinese faith. In addition to the village's longstanding reputation as a centre of fine arts, it is Ubud's active, aesthetically spectacular spirituality that is one of its biggest drawcards. Whatever time of year you visit, you will probably find that there's a celebration, parade or festival that you are welcome to observe and even take part in. That's why Ubud remains a favourite destination for travellers who want to experience Bali's culture as well as the sunshine.

Uma Ubud is the most recent address in Ubud to open its doors, and the travel press in particular was keen to see what Christina Ong – already an innovator with her Metropolitan

hotels in London and Bangkok and her retreat destinations in the Maldives (Cocoa Island) and the Caribbean (Parrot Cay) – would do in Bali's number one village. People who are expecting something mindbogglingly different will be disappointed. Uma Ubud does not knock you off your feet with the shock of the new. In fact, at first glance, it seems to have repeated many ingredients that you would think of as 'classic' Ubud: the villas with roofs thatched in alang alang grass, which cascade down a valley towards a river; the stand-alone reception; the dining area as a lofty, open pavilion constructed in teak pillars; the frangipani trees; or the flagstone paths on green lawns. None of these are new or unusual to the area – and neither were they meant to be.

The design approach was to create a contemporary setting that surprises with sophisticated subtlety rather than brazen boldness. Chances are that on a casual twenty-minute visit, you probably wouldn't take in the collective creativity that makes Uma Ubud

special. You wouldn't notice, for instance, the variety of funky, custom-made paper lamps that decorate the villas by Japanese interior designer Koichiro Ikebuchi. Nor would you see the shiny all-black bathrooms divided from the all-white sleeping pavilions by very Zen water gardens. And unless you came by at night, you'd also be likely to miss the installation of contemporary lanterns that illuminate the open dining space, a series of ultra-simple glass orbs suspended at different heights to create intriguing patterns.

The new-generation, Isamu Noguchi-style lamps, the pale, lime-washed interiors, the polished black bathrooms, the spill pool that forms a wall of water for pedestrians below, the massive stone sculpture that separates the reception from the pool… all of these aesthetic factors have much more to do with refinement than innovation. And that's what makes Uma so perfect for Ubud. Not only is it in tune with its location; it's also in tune with its spirit.

---

address Uma Ubud, Jalan Raya Sanggingan, Banjar Lungsiakan, Kedewatan, Ubud, 80571 Bali, Indonesia
t +62 (0)361 972 448   **f** +62 (0)361 972 449   **e** info.ubud@uma.como.bz
room rates from US$205

puri ganesha

'The trouble is, they never want to come over the mountain. Once they do, they're always happy they did.' So says Diana von Cranach, the pioneering, distinctly eccentric and slightly outrageous proprietor of Puri Ganesha.

Few people realize that Bali is divided into north and south by a massive mountain range. Ubud, for most, is as far north as they venture, and yet in geographical terms it's still in the south. Cutting across the middle of the island is a series of mountainous peaks that rise to the not insubstantial height of seven thousand feet. It's a spectacular and often overlooked part of Bali's geography. The three freshwater lakes, empty craters of dormant volcanoes, are worth the effort in their own right. But another reward awaits the intrepid traveller: the quiet, almost undiscovered north coast of Bali. Though the drive is not more than four hours from Denpasar, visitors and guides tend to have a mental block about the north; traffic to the area consists mainly of locals, from truck drivers, buses and work crews to people heading south for the shopping. There are no supermarkets, restaurants, surf shops or bikini boutiques on this side of the island. And for many that's precisely the attraction.

But Bali's north is not just a quieter, less developed version of the south. The high mountains divide more than just the land. The north is far more arid than the south, and even in the wet season it hardly ever rains here. The land is usually much less green, and the hills are a dusty brown punctuated by the odd tree. For many Europeans and Americans who already see their fair share of rain, the weather on Bali's northwestern coast is ideal.

Sun, privacy and quiet are three things English expat von Cranach can guarantee at Puri Ganesha. She has built an exceptional series of beachside villas on an isolated stretch of this northern coast. Though the property describes itself as a hotel, it shares little with the established sense of the word. You get a house, a butler and a housekeeper, and as a guest you make the decisions regarding not just what and when to eat, but also where. There are no formal restaurants or even public spaces, and you're left with the impression that you have simply retreated to your own secluded, fully staffed villa.

But, you may ask, what is there to do here besides the obvious, i.e. nothing at all? For starters, some of the best snorkelling in the region is just off the beach. What's more,

The mountains of Bali's seldom-visited north provide a spectacular backdrop to Puri Ganesha's beachfront location.

Black-and-white check is an important textile pattern in Bali; locals use it to decorate their shrines.

Large and beautifully illuminated loft-style bedrooms occupy the entire top floor of each Puri Ganesha villa.

Colour, texture and gilded detail –
the design of Puri Ganesha
is rich in tradition.

Every villa has its own swimming pool
paved in the distinctive green-
coloured local stone.

Open on three sides, the veranda on the
upper floor of each villa offers a superb
view of sunrise on the Bali Sea.

Puri Ganesha is only a forty-five-minute ferry ride away from the unexplored eastern tip of Java. For the culturally aware tourist, the place is an endless source of undiscovered bounty, and treasure-hunting is one of the activities von Cranach excels at. The kind of expeditions she leads into Java are of the shopping variety. Colonial antiques, Javanese handcrafts, monumental seashells, traditional textiles… the serious souvenir hunter, decorator or serial house renovator will find von Cranach a world-class guide to all of these.

Pemuteran, the village where Puri Ganesha is situated, is a magical place. The question is, how did a white English woman who lived most of her adult life in Cologne end up here? Von Cranach first came to Bali in 1984 with her husband, a German economist, and loved it so much that she had an inkling even then that one day she would live here. By 1987 she was serious enough about moving to 'paradise' to start looking for some land. In those days most expats lived in and around Seminyak, and tourism was mainly centred around Nusa Dua, Kuta Beach and Ubud; any mention of Pemuteran would have had most residents, including the Balinese themselves, racing to a map. Yet it was here that von Cranach had been told of a large parcel of absolute beachfront – a rare commodity in Bali. She dutifully journeyed to the north with a friend, only to find a place that completely underwhelmed her. 'It's awful,' said her companion, 'so dry, so desolate, so isolated – I'd kill myself here.' And then the spirits intervened. In a moment of New Age clarity worthy of Shirley MacLaine, she tripped and ended up face down in the black sand, convinced that forces were commanding her to stay. She bought the land and then did nothing with it for almost ten years. Once again, fate played a hand. Her marriage broke up, and she took off with a suitcase and two hundred Deutschmarks, determined to make something of her Bali beachfront. Puri Ganesha is the result.

address Puri Ganesha Villas, Desa Pemuteran, Gerokgak, Singaraja 8115, Bali, Indonesia
t +62 (0)362 94 766 **f** +62 (0)362 93 433 **e** pganesha@indosat.net.id
room rates from US$423

ibrik

An *ibrik* is a small container for pouring coffee. It's a Turkish word. It's also the smallest urban Hip Hotel in Asia, with three rooms and a café on the banks of Bangkok's Chao Phraya River. Three rooms hardly seem worth the effort – for the proprietor, that is. But for the guest it's a fantastic opportunity, a chance to experience the hustle and bustle of Bangkok without feeling like one of thousands of *farang* (foreign) tourists. Ibrik's guestrooms are spacious and decorated in a modern, 'look what I managed to do with my family hand-me-downs' kind of way. They are also immaculately tidy and comprehensively contemporary, especially in the bathroom department. It's like staying with a cool friend on the river. The only other accommodation options on the Chao Phraya consist of expensive institutional hotels such as the Oriental; these may indulge you with four-star luxury but cannot match Ibrik for raw, full-on authenticity.

The river, once the lifeblood of the city, is now less used for transport. You can still catch a ferry across it for 2 baht (less than a cent), and for 400 baht you can hire a *rua hang yao*, a narrow long-tailed boat powered by an exposed car engine sticking out the back, which moves passengers up and down the *klongs*

(canals) at high speed. The sheer magic of Ibrik is you can sit on your terrace, which is literally hanging over the river, and watch this fascinating city go by – without the claustrophobic feeling of being trapped in your hotel room. Ibrik is not a place where you will be left with a sense of having spent two nights in Bangkok and not seen a thing, even if you hardly venture out. It's perfect for the less motivated among us: it has its own café so you won't starve if you refuse to leave the premises, but if you do, you have plenty of other options at your doorstep that won't involve an itinerary discussion with a concierge.

As might be expected of such an original inn, Ibrik is not a product of a hotel culture. It was the idea of three young, like-minded creative types who could see a complete lack of smaller, more colourful places to stay in this Asian metropolis. Gobe Bunnag is a professional photographer, and the house that is now Ibrik used to belong to friends of hers. When the building came on the market, she and her partners saw their window of opportunity. The interesting thing is that Ibrik doesn't feel like a three-room hotel at all. Perhaps it's the professional way it's run, or the fact that the rooms are so far apart, or the manner in which the café co-exists seamlessly with the accommodation. In fact, it feels more like a hotel with twenty rooms, and yet you have the distinct advantage of knowing that you'll never have to share the common areas with more than five other people.

In a sense, the history of Bangkok is the history of the river that runs through it. It was here on the east bank of the Chao Phraya that King Buddha Yodfa Chulaloke or Rama I, the first king of the Chakri Dynasty that still reigns today, established the new capital of Siam in 1782. The previous capital, Ayutthaya, had existed for 417 years, and when it was destroyed by Burmese invaders in 1767, the shock was analogous to France losing Paris. Initially, Rama I chose for the new capital to be situated on a river so that he could easily escape from danger. As his kingdom strengthened, however, and his troops successfully repelled Burmese invasion, the role of the river shifted as it became a defensive barrier as opposed to a means of escape. A massive palace and temple were built at a strategically defensible location and the entire city was encircled by a network of klongs allowing for quick, efficient troop transfer. Sadly, most of the klongs have now been filled in as a result of more than a century of growth and development, but in reality the waterways were only ever used for trade, earning Bangkok the reputation of the Venice of the East. As it turned out, Rama I and his successors were such capable diplomats that Thailand became the only Southeast Asian nation never to be colonized. Today, Bangkok is recognized as one of the most modern cities in Asia, but like the Thames in London or the Seine in Paris, the Chao Phraya is still an integral part of the city, even if its practical function has declined.

With Ibrik your Bangkok adventure can start virtually on landing at the airport. Instead of sitting in traffic looking at billboards featuring football stars flogging Pepsi, you simply head straight to the river and arrive by boat.

address Ibrik Resort, 256 Soi Wat Rakang, Arunamrin Road, Bangkoknoi, Bangkok 10700, Thailand
t +66 (0)2 848 9220 **f** +66 (0)2 411 1183 **e** info@ibrikresort.com
room rates from Baht 3,200

the metropolitan

It takes quite a stretch of imagination to stand in the middle of an immense badminton hall and see it as a series of luxurious penthouse suites. But that's exactly how Bangkok's Metropolitan came about: it used to be the YMCA. In fact, most taxi drivers still know it as such. Jump into any cab in Bangkok, ask to be taken to the Metropolitan and 10 to 1 you'll draw a blank. Yet Sathorn Road is one of the best-known streets in the city. The safest way to guarantee you'll get there is to tell the driver that you want to go to the old YMCA.

As one of the most dynamic cities in Asia, Bangkok today has little to do with temples, palaces or kickboxing. People in search of the exotic land of Buddhas and gilded royal barges will be disappointed. Elephants no longer play a role in everyday life and people are more likely to be found sitting behind a desk than wading in a rice paddy. Of all the hotels in Bangkok, the Metropolitan is the first in step with the city's new energy and direction. Bangkok's restaurants, bars, nightclubs and bookstores testify to its appetite for the cutting edge and the contemporary; the city is embracing modernity, looking to the future without worrying too much about what's being left behind.

The Metropolitan is a three-dimensional metaphor for the city itself. Unapologetically modern but distinctively Asian, the hotel presents a heady combination of the cool and contemporary with re-invented tradition. The aesthetic of the 166 rooms, 4 penthouse suites and duplex presidential suite is a pared-down mix of East meets West. Acres of dark Thai *makha* timber for the floors and furniture in teak are combined with one-off pieces by up-and-coming Thai artist Natee Utarit and an ultra-slick lighting scheme from London's Isometrix. The interiors are the work of Singapore-based Kathryn Kng, billed as Singapore's hottest interior designer, who has certainly given the Metropolitan's owner Christina Ong visual value for her money, particularly in the double-storey lobby and the blue-detailed restaurant Cy'an. Asia's answer to Nobu, Cy'an serves some of the best and most inventive food in Bangkok. And in step with the new culinary wave in Asia, its chef Amanda Gale comes from Australia. After working for almost a decade with Neil Perry from Sydney's famous Rockpool (the restaurant often credited with pioneering fusion cuisine), Gale arrived in Bangkok following a stint at Parrot Cay in the Turks and Caicos Islands. The thing about

Cy'an is that it's a serious restaurant in a laid-back space, which is typical of the way Christina Ong and her company COMO Hotels & Resorts are redefining what's important in the contemporary hotel experience; it's a fashionably relaxed approach to upmarket accommodation that continues with the rooms.

More like private lofts than conventional hotel rooms, they are the property's real *tour-de-force*. The bathrooms, for instance, are configured in such a way that they're flooded with natural daylight, unlike the artificially lit caves you find elsewhere. Light, space and modernity – the Metropolitan is a symbol of Asia's growing creative confidence. With staff uniforms designed by Yohji Yamomoto, guestrooms that feel more like a downtown studio than a box, understated splashes of Jim Thompson silk, a gym that is not just an afterthought, an alternative health food restaurant called Glow and COMO's trendsetting Shambhala spa, it's more than just a look that sets this hotel apart. It follows

a clearly conceived philosophy of modern luxury that is the cornerstone of all COMO properties worldwide. The Metropolitan in London, Coco Island in the Maldives, Uma Ubud in Bali and indeed the Metropolitan in Bangkok may not appear to have anything in common, but they are united in a commitment to certain core values: namely, clean, crisp design expressed in the vernacular vocabulary of the location, combined with the recuperative and relaxing qualities offered by the spa and its signature treatments. Although subtle, these elements represent a complete shift in what people would normally associate with a city hotel; guests here are more likely to spend their time in the juice bar than the bar.

Unlike traditional hotels that smother you with 'fattening' luxury, the Metropolitan in Bangkok makes sure you leave looking better than when you arrived. It's all about looking and feeling good in a five-star environment that still lets you have breakfast in your board-shorts.

address The Metropolitan, 27 South Sathorn Road, Tungmahamek, Sathorn, Bangkok 10120, Thailand

t +66 (0)2 625 3333 **f** +66 (0)2 625 3300 **e** res.bkk@metropolitan.como.bz

room rates from US$240

the china club

Crouching Tiger, Hidden Dragon. These were the first words a friend in Hong Kong used to describe the China Club in Beijing. 'You'll love it,' she said. 'It's just like staying in the film but with great food.' And she was right.

Situated down a quiet *hutong* (typical Beijing lane) not far from the Forbidden City and Tiananmen Square, this former palace has changed very little since it was built in the seventeenth century for a son of Emperor Kang Xi of the Qing Dynasty. Remarkably, virtually all of its architectural features have survived intact. This no doubt has a lot to do with the fact that for four decades it housed one of the best restaurants in Beijing – it was the favourite Szechuan kitchen of Deng Xiao Ping, the Chairman of the Communist Party post-Mao. Eventually, however, despite the restaurant's reputation and stellar clientele, at one hundred thousand-plus square feet (divided into countless smaller dining rooms), it was too large to sustain, particularly in the newly competitive post-Communism Beijing. Even the patronage of the country's number one leader was no longer enough.

When the opportunity arose a decade ago to take over this historic property, Hong Kong-based tycoon, art collector and fashion entrepreneur David Tang didn't hesitate. An extensive but sensitive renovation project was embarked upon and completed so successfully that it's impossible to spot such giveaways of modernity as airconditioning units, even though there's one in every dining room.

The true beauty of the place is the way it's divided into pavilions. Everywhere you go, there's another hidden courtyard, private dining room or secret bar. Design-wise, Tang has nonetheless adhered to the idea of a club, a supper club that also happens to have some very smart overnight accommodation. Best of all, if you stay here there's really not much reason to go out because the China Club plays host to one of Beijing's most successful 'scenes'. Every evening at around 7pm, an entire convoy of shiny black limousines with tinted windows pulls into the cramped first courtyard. Elegantly dressed ladies of leisure, fat captains of industry and the odd media glamourpuss step out into the almost film-set environment of the Beijing China Club. Even though the surrounding towers of glass and steel serve as a reminder of the new dimensions of China's capital, there's still something distinctly nostalgic about the

whole experience. The China Club is chic, cosmopolitan and decadent, in a 1920s Shanghai sort of way; it's a place for long, silk *cheongsam* dresses split at the side and sober black suits.

What is perhaps most impressive about the China Club, apart from the fact that it has managed to survive both the Communist and Cultural Revolutions, is its seductive use of colour. We always associate China with the colour red, but traditional Chinese interiors are far more multicoloured than you'd expect. At the China Club, yellow, purple, royal blue, light blue, cream, black, orange and green – chartreuse, olive and lime – all feature as part of the decorative palette, along with plenty of gilding. Yet despite the profusion of colour, it has been used in a deliberate and systematic manner. Colour guides you from one space to the next, and distinguishes one room from another. Within the private dining rooms, the chromatic schemes are pared down to two or three hues. There is, for instance, a yellow

dining room accented with purple silk and dark timber, just as there is a cream-coloured private dining room with black furniture and splashes of green and orange.

In the guestrooms, colour has been limited to dark red or chartreuse green Chairman Mao-style club seats in bouclé velvet with white lace armrests. These rooms are unlike any you're likely to have been in before. The bed is hidden in its own alcove in the centre of the space, divided from the living room and the bathroom by corridors created with Chinese-patterned timber trellis panels that also provide a decorative focus. The effect is reminiscent of the film *Raise the Red Lantern*. There is nothing vaguely 'hotel room' about these suites, and even the towels break vividly with tradition. Hotel towels are almost always white or cream. At the China Club they're bright pink. Never did I think I'd be walking around in a pink bathrobe, but such is the power of a mysterious and seductive environment.

address The China Club Beijing, 51 Xi Rong Xian Lane, Xi Dan, Beijing, China
t +86 (0)10 6603 8855 **f** +86 (0)10 6603 9594 **e** tccbadmn@public.bta.net.cn
room rates from US$108

uma paro

Of all the places I was looking forward to visiting for this book, Bhutan was on top of the list. Who wouldn't jump at the chance to visit the last Buddhist kingdom on earth?

Bhutan, the tiny nation in the Himalayas that lies between India to the south and Tibet to the north, is widely acknowledged as one of the few places in the world that has not been spoilt by tourism. It is by all accounts 'authentic'. How authentic? Most of the population of one million still wear traditional dress, and the entire country is so devoutly Buddhist that no one would consider buying so much as a goat cart without getting it blessed at a monastery. Society in general is still almost completely agrarian: most people farm for a living, and virtually the only other occupation is to be a monk. Practically every majestically steep hillside has a temple clinging to it, while the valleys are dominated by farms and barns. It sounds like Switzerland, you may say – except that whereas the Swiss live in a modern, technologically advanced state, the Bhutanese live in a positively medieval one. This is a land of hand tools and wooden-wheeled transport. People are simple: they love their land, their Buddha and their king; they have no computers, cars or electronic conveniences;

they don't rely on television for entertainment; and their lives aren't complicated by credit cards or mortgages.

No wonder, then, that most stories about Bhutan ring seductively of Shangri-la, the legendary paradise the world has somehow forgotten. In 1974 the country had fewer than 300 visitors; by 2000 this figure had expanded to 7,500, but that's still less than the number of people that British Airways flies to New York from London in a day. This has a lot to do with the king, His Majesty Jigme Singye Wangchuk, who is simply not interested in raising the number of tourists. Instead, he is committed to a policy of encouraging small numbers of high-paying travellers to visit the country. This may sound elitist, but the truth is that quality of experience has always been linked to price. What does it cost, for instance, to participate in an Arctic expedition? Certain things and places have to be protected to be preserved, and Bhutan is one of them.

That's where Uma Paro comes in. Situated in a long, spectacular, pine-clad valley with a river snaking through it, Paro is one of the cultural centres of Bhutan; the town is flanked by rice paddies, wheat fields and trout-filled streams, and the thirty-eight-acre site of Uma

Paro is on a nearby hill. As one of two highly regarded travel entrepreneurs to be invited into the hermit kingdom of Bhutan, Christina Ong used her entry to introduce the second of her new brand of hotels to open in Asia (the first is Uma Ubud in Bali). The concept behind Uma (which means 'living home' in Bahasha) is straightforward: to offer a contemporary environment imbued with local ingredients so that the guest feels simultaneously at home and somewhere new. Architecturally, Uma Paro comprises twenty rooms and nine villas, one of which is rumoured to have been booked by Sting long before the hotel was even finished. Creatively speaking, one thing is clear: a lot of hard work went into ensuring that this property would deliver both the vibrancy of the local vernacular and the contemporary style and comfort travellers have grown to expect – it's Bhutanese enough to be different and comfortable enough to be desirable. To accomplish the task, an international team of talent was assembled. Singapore-based Malaysian Cheong Yew Kwan, best known for his work on Begawan Giri, was brought in for the architecture. With Uma Paro, he opted for a style suggestive of a utilitarian Bhutanese farm dwelling, and the building materials – stone, wood and tiles – are no different from what the locals have been using for ages (literally). The meticulous concern for incorporating Bhutanese elements continues in the interior design of Kathryn Kng, who has set timber darkened by smoke from wood fires against white walls vividly handpainted with flowers, birds and spiritual motifs by local artists; the theme extends to the furniture made from *shesham*, a local wood.

From the handstitched bed covers in Bhutanese colours to the handwoven Nepalese rugs to the traditional *bukhari* fireplaces, the emphasis is on cosy, comfortable and colourful, without compromising a sense of space. Uma Paro is the result of a gigantic effort to measure up to Bhutan's naive charm, native beauty and comprehensive authenticity.

---

address Uma Paro, P.O. Box 222, Paro, Bhutan

t +975 8 271 597   **f** +975 8 271 513   **e** info.paro@uma.como.bz

room rates from US$210

amankora

'Honey, look at this place in Tibet. It looks fabulous! I'd love to go to Tibet; wouldn't you? It sounds so exotic.' The couple sitting behind me on the flight from Phuket to Bangkok had just stayed at Amanpuri. I knew they'd had a brochure on Amankora slipped into the envelope containing their bill because I had the same in mine. The woman went on and on about Tibet, and I was sorely tempted to turn around and politely inform her that Bhutan and Tibet are not one and the same. In the end, though, I decided against it. Who could blame her, after all? How many people have even heard of Bhutan, let alone know where it is?

Wedged in the Himalayas between India, Nepal and China, this tiny kingdom was completely cut off from the rest of the world until the late 1960s. Its people, devout Buddhists all, have been living in a manner that has changed little in the past millennium. The country's rich geography spans subtropical plains, densely forested alpine valleys and windswept, snow-covered peaks, and its wildlife includes the elusive snow leopard, the golden langur (whatever that is), blue sheep, tigers, water buffalo, elephants and yaks. But who would know? Bhutan remains one of the world's last secrets, and that's what made it

such a desirable prize for hotel and travel entrepreneur Adrian Zecha. For anyone who has travelled a great deal, discovering the place that no one has ever been is, of course, the ultimate challenge. Zecha was on the inaugural Druk Air flight to Bhutan from Bangkok in 1987, and for him it was love at first sight. Smitten with the country and burning with the desire to develop a resort there, he waged a ten-year campaign of lobbying with the government to allow him to put an Aman in Bhutan. As it turned out, Zecha's plans dovetailed perfectly with the vision of King Jigme Singye Wangchuk, who has been carefully guiding his country to prosperity since 1972.

Getting the green light was one thing; making it happen was another. But in the past, this has been something of a recurring theme wherever Aman has decided to plant its flag. Bhutan, however, proved to be that much more difficult because the locals have always been entirely self-sufficient. Try explaining to people who have always built their own houses, grown their own food and raised their own farm animals why others should have it all done for them. The complete absence of technology in Bhutan didn't help either.

The staff, for instance, tried to use a vacuum cleaner to heat food, and they greeted the blue-light fly zapper in the kitchen with howls of despair because it's against Buddhist doctrine to kill any living thing, no matter how small. Even the guest menu became a cultural issue because the decision to ease up on the chili content was seen as offensive – the locals eat a lot of chili, and it seemed distinctly dishonest to them to serve so-called Bhutanese cuisine that in their opinion didn't taste Bhutanese. Nevertheless, the perseverance that has seen Aman emerge victoriously in other so-called difficult markets such as Morocco, India and Indonesia ensured that they were able to open a lodge in Paro in the summer of 2004. It should have been a substantial feather in Zecha's cap, but this was only the beginning. Zecha's vision for Bhutan is to open a series of six small lodges – all named Amankora – throughout the kingdom, which will enable an extraordinary tour of discovery, with guests never having to sleep in anything other than an Aman. It is a spectacularly ambitious plan, especially since some of the prospective sites lack roads, while others such as the picturesque Punakha can only be reached by crossing a raging river.

All in all, it reads like a story from *Tin Tin in Tibet*, but I'm sure that the legendary willpower of Mr Zecha will prevail. In the meantime, guests have to make do with the lodge in Paro – by all accounts no great sacrifice. Each of the twenty-four suites is true to the Aman signature: luxurious, spacious, uncluttered and streamlined, and designed in a manner sympathetic to the location. At Amankora, the Bhutanese ingredients include walls made of rammed earth and a wood-burning bukhari stove in every room. It's true that there's still the odd logistical glitch, such as massive landslides blocking the access road that brings supplies from India, but one thing is certain: this is the first Aman where the experience is as much of an adventure for the staff as it is for the guests.

address Amankora, Paro, Bhutan
t +975 8 240 200 **f** +975 8 240 201 **e** info@amanresorts.com
room rates from US$925

la résidence d'angkor

The most puzzling thing about the ruins of Angkor is how little survives of the day-to-day existence of the people of the Khmer Empire, which flourished for over five hundred years and at its height covered the whole of present-day Cambodia and most of Thailand. There's nothing: not a house, book, jewel, domestic implement nor single item of clothing. Most of what we know about everyday Khmer culture comes from the carvings and inscriptions in the temples it left behind. It's a bit like learning the culture of Europeans solely from a few surviving cathedrals (a scary thought indeed).

A Khmer temple was not a meeting place for the faithful like a church, mosque or synagogue; it was the palace of a god. A god such as Vishnu had the power of beneficence, both here and in the hereafter, and the more beautiful his palace, the happier (and more generous) he would be. Gods took the form of statues in the temples, and it was the duty of devotees to tend to them: for instance, they would dress them, adorn them with jewelry and bring them offerings of food, flowers and incense at least three times a day. At Angkor, the scale of this work was in line with the scale of the temples, i.e. huge. From an inscription in the ruins of Ta Prohm (featured in the movie

Tomb Raider), we learn that in the twelfth century this temple complex was serviced by almost thirteen thousand monks, and its maintenance required the toil and produce of another eighty thousand people in the various villages that belonged to it.

Whereas today the temples are impressive but austere, they would have been lively and crowded in their heyday. The area between the outer wall and the temple itself would have been packed with small wooden structures on stilts. The statues would have been covered in the finest silks and adorned with the most exquisite jewelry, while the corridors filled with the smell of incense and the to-ing and fro-ing of shaven-headed, saffron-clad monks. The most colourful player in Angkor life would have been the king, whose every movement was accompanied by tremendous pageantry. Zhou Daguan, a Chinese envoy who visited Angkor in 1296, wrote a unique eyewitness account of the spectacle of the Khmer king's entourage in his *Memoirs on the Customs of Cambodia*: 'When the King leaves his palace the procession is headed by cavalry – then come the flags, the banners and the music. Three to five hundred gaily dressed palace girls, with flowers in their hair and tapers in

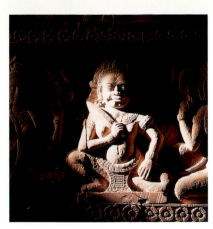

Stone murals at La Résidence d'Angkor mimic the carved galleries of nearby Angkor Wat.

La Résidence is in Siem Reap, the town adjacent to Angkor Wat, which hosts a large population of Buddhist monks.

Vast expanses of teak are punctuated by walls of carved stone at one of Southeast Asia's most handsome hotels.

Angkor's monumental treasures were built by Hindus – the Khmer converted to Buddhism many centuries later.

At the peak of the Khmer Empire, even kings lived in wooden palaces; stone structures were reserved for the gods.

Buddhist monks look after the statues in the temple – they are the valets of the gods.

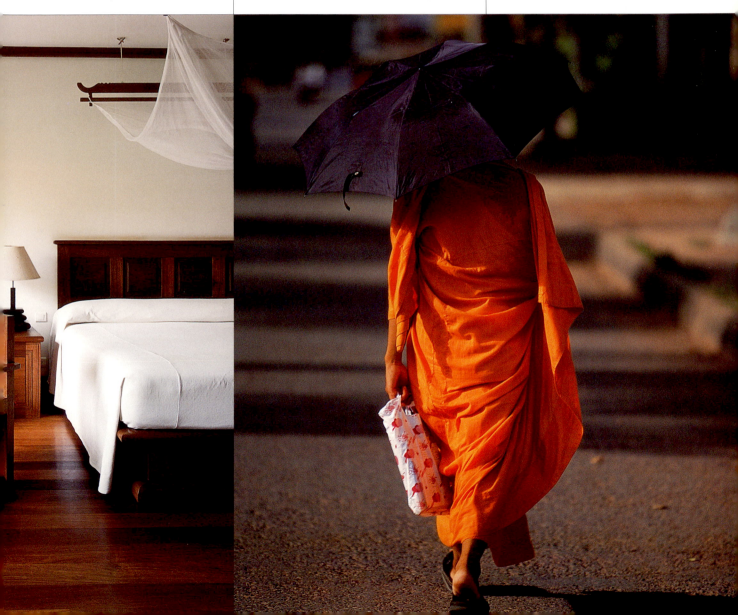

their hands, are massed together in a separate group.... Following them come chariots drawn by goats and horses, all adorned with gold.... Finally the Sovereign appears, standing erect on an elephant....'

Apart from the temples made of stone (a material reserved exclusively for the dwellings of gods), all Khmer architecture was built in wood. Even the king lived in a wooden palace, albeit a very grand one with a tiled roof. It's therefore appropriate that the Pansea Orient-Express Hotels group opted for wood when choosing a stylistic approach for their Angkor property. La Résidence d'Angkor, in the heart of the small but pretty tree-lined town of Siem Reap, is an exotic, dark-wooden-panelled escape from the heat and bustle of outdoors. The minute you enter the building, you feel the soothing effects of your surroundings. Although La Résidence is very affordable, it certainly doesn't look it. For starters, there's the pool, a sumptuous 130-foot-long stretch of emerald green tiles with two Hindu-inspired fountains.

The guest rooms continue the theme of both dark wood – for the floors and the furniture – and the luxury of space, with bathrooms the size of an average hotel room in Paris. The decor combines an earthy Asian signature with a contemporary flourish: dark timber and white walls are punctuated by splashes of vividly coloured Cambodian silks used as tablecloths and pillows throughout the hotel.

Without fail, most newcomers to Angkor are impressed by La Résidence's two-storey teak lobby and the moat you cross to get to it. But don't forget, they haven't been to the temples yet. And that's the point of Angkor. You go there to marvel at the engineering feats of the Khmer Empire, to consider the sheer number of magnificent temples they constructed and the complexity of the waterworks they created on such a monumental scale. The beauty of La Résidence is in its architectural continuity. Then and now, people visiting stone temples dedicated to Vishnu return to houses built entirely in wood.

---

address La Résidence d'Angkor, River Road, Siem Reap, Cambodia

t +855 (0)63 963 390 **f** +855 (0)63 963 391 **e** angkor@pansea.com

room rates from US$205

amansara

When visiting dignitaries such as Brezhnev, Ho Chi Minh or Jackie Kennedy were invited to Siem Reap in the early 1960s for a private tour of the temples of Angkor, they would be put up in the guest villa of Prince Norodom Sihanouk (later the King of Cambodia). Architecturally speaking, the two worlds couldn't have been more opposite. Known then as the Villa Princière, Prince Sihanouk's pad was a white-walled compound of modernist reinforced concrete. Designed by French architect Laurent Mondet and completed in 1962, it was and still is a sleek collection of low horizontal lines and capacious circular domes. Angkor, on the other hand, is a riot of Hindu shapes, figures and carvings, executed in acre after acre of solid sandstone.

On a pragmatic level, Prince Sihanouk had understood that there was no competing with Angkor Wat's exotic grandeur. He had also guessed, quite wisely, that after a day spent visiting the area's temples and monuments, guests might welcome a retreat into a soothing absence of decorativeness. And though nowadays he no longer owns or runs it, his villa continues to operate in the same contrast-rich style. Amansara's clean, sixties-inspired lines have more in common with Frank Sinatra's Palm

Springs than with Jayavarman's VII's great capital of the mighty Khmer empire. Exploring the monumental remains left behind by a succession of Khmer kings is a strenuous pastime, and the hotel's groovy modernist aesthetic hasn't lost its appeal as a haven from Angkor's Hindu hype.

Angkor Wat is a Caligula-style feast of statistics, covering over five hundred acres of land – the surrounding moat alone is over six hundred feet wide and nearly four miles long. Built during the reign of King Suryavarman II in the first half of the twelfth century, the great complex was originally dedicated to the god Vishnu, striving through its architecture to create a microcosm of the Hindu universe (although it has since been converted to Buddhist practice). Its quintet of conical towers mimics the five heavenly peaks of Mount Meru and, to emphasize the rewards of heavenly life, the structure is adorned with carvings of over 1,800 *apsaras* (celestial maidens). But the most remarkable artistry lies in the galleries that run around the whole temple. These seemingly never-ending 'tapestries' of beautifully executed, intricately detailed bas-reliefs depict scenes from Hindu mythology and civic lore, covering the gambit of human experience.

To take in all the stories told by these figurative visual feasts would take many, many days – more time than most visitors have. That said, the greatest mistake that many travellers to Angkor make is not allowing enough time. It's impossible to visit Siem Reap successfully in just two days, no matter how determined or dedicated you are to the task. That's because Angkor Wat is only part of the picture. There are also – to name just a few – Bantheai Srei, Preah Khan, Ta Prohm and Neak Pean, not to mention Angkor Thom, the great town within whose walls the Khmer kings resided. And central to Angkor Thom is one of the most striking structures in the religious world, the temple of Bayon, composed of a collection of fifty-four massive stone towers, each carved in the shape of the smiling face of Buddha.

Simply put, Angkor is overwhelming, and Amansara's pristine sixties-inspired modernism with an Asian twist is just what you need after the carved cacophony of the Khmer temples.

Architect Kerry Hill's renovation of the Villa Princière is comfortable, clever and appropriate. He has taken the 1960s as a starting point and introduced furniture inspired by Jean Prouvé, executed in the distinctly Asian materials of teak and raffia. But it's the scale of Amansara that makes it so comfortable: it retains the feel of staying in someone's villa, without the occasional headache of having to be nice to the host. And yet because it's an Aman, the level of service creates the impression that you're the only one there.

From black-and-white snapshots taken when it first opened, it's clear that not all that much has changed since the Prince welcomed visitors here; the round dining room, for instance, is the same space used in the same way. But the place benefits hugely from the Aman group's commitment to aesthetic perfection. Guests lounge by the pool in Californian Palm Springs fashion; it's just that here the golf courses are (thankfully) replaced by the world's most captivating temples.

---

address Amansara, Road to Angkor, Siem Reap, Cambodia

t +855 (0)63 760 333 **f** +855 (0)63 760 335 **e** amansara@amanresorts.com

room rates from US$700

fcc

Now is the time to travel to Cambodia to experience Angkor Wat. The adjacent town of Siem Reap is still small, pretty and unspoilt, the nearby international airport is only an hour's flight from Bangkok and, better still, the monuments are not yet overwhelmed by tourists. Plus, just as importantly, visitors have some interesting choices of accommodation.

FCC is for travellers who like their colonial atmosphere pared down and contemporary. Set in the grounds of a former French governer's holiday home, it combines a shuttered two-storey structure typical of French Indochina with modern bungalows that face either the park or the pool. Polished concrete floors, the odd fifties-inspired rattan chair, open-plan bathrooms and splashes of Cambodian silk constitute the decorative picture. Simple and coolly confident, FCC's interiors and bold geometric architecture make for an unexpectedly attractive package.

Central to the hotel is the original French colonial building, which now houses a restaurant, a shop and a couple of bars. Once the headquarters of the Cambodian police, it reminds me of the building in the movie *The Killing Fields* to which the foreign correspondents, photographers and embassy workers retreat when the Khmer Rouge take over Phnom Penh. I went back to that film after visiting Cambodia, trying to understand how a country of people capable of creating beauty the likes of Angkor could have ended up on such a senselessly destructive path. The Khmer Rouge introduced the country to the twisted concept of auto-genocide, and almost succeeded. *The Killing Fields* is sad and powerful, and it brings home just how far this nation has managed to claw its way back from the absolute edge. It's hard to believe that today's Cambodia is the same nation. People are open, friendly and polite (even airport security staff apologize for having to look through your bags), everything is tidy, workers are efficient and quick to catch on, and service is on a par with the finest places in Asia.

For travellers, the most tangible benefit of the new, politically stable Cambodia is that the complex of Angkor is once again open to visitors. Some Westerners such as German photographer Jaroslav Poncar journeyed here while the Khmer Rouge were still in power; Poncar tells stories of how he had to time his camera exposures to coincide with the intervals between mortar explosions. Most people, however, have waited for the dust to settle. It's evident from the building activity on the outskirts of Siem Reap that the government is confident that Angkor will flourish as a destination. While that's good news for the Cambodian economy, it spells the end of any chance of having the ruins to yourself. At the moment, though, it's still possible to wander around some of the temples in relative peace. Consider, for instance, Ta Prohm, the site that for many visitors leaves the strongest impression. It's a place of fantasy that brings out the Indiana Jones in us all: overgrown by forest and entangled with the gigantic, octopus-like roots of the kapok tree, Ta Prohm provides an insight into what Frenchman Henri Mouhot and other explorers must have felt when they first stumbled onto the remains of the capital of what was once the mightiest empire in Southeast Asia. Here you are free to discover the ruins on your own, without guides, cassettes or roped-off areas. I was completely alone in this vast complex when a small Cambodian boy, impressed by my camera, took it upon himself to show me every location used for the movie *Tomb Raider*. These turned out to be graphic examples of nature reasserting the upper hand, but the real drama came from the imagination being allowed to roam without rules or regulations.

At night, the scene transfers back to town. Aside from FCC's colonial charm and avant-garde architecture, it's one of the best hangouts in Siem Reap. There's an outdoor bar with a collection of Art Deco armchairs of the kind that used to furnish every hall of commerce in the time of Chairman Mao; and upstairs there are two restaurants under a formidable installation of ceiling fans, where you can eat while watching the town's traffic of motorized rickshaws going back and forth.

From a historical, psychological and financial point of view, FCC is an interesting approach to a hotel. The atmosphere recalls a colonial setting, the style is confidently contemporary and the prices belong to a forgotten era.

address FCC Angkor, Pokambor Avenue (next to the Royal Residence), Siem Reap, Cambodia

t +855 (0)63 760 280   **f** +855 (0)63 760 281   **e** angkor@fcccambodia.com

room rates from US$90

commune by the great wall

Even if you only have a passing interest in contemporary architecture, you could not have failed to notice the new revolution in the People's Republic of China – a design revolution. Beijing is busy reinventing itself, and not in a small or conservative manner. The types of buildings cutting-edge architects normally only dream of getting built are being built. There's the hundred-thousand-seat stadium for the 2008 Olympics, for instance, by Swiss architectural duo Herzog & de Meuron, a sports palace of sorts cocooned in a bird's nest of tangled steel and twisted columns. Or Dutch architect Rem Koolhaas's O-shaped skyscraper for Chinese state television network CCTV, a monumental reminder of the play possibilites of Lego. What with a Zaha Hadid scheme for downtown residential towers and a new dragon-shaped airport by London's Norman Foster in the planning, China is poised to be the new grande dame of avant-garde architecture.

Even on a smaller scale, new architectural possibilities are being explored. The Commune by the Great Wall is a powerful and intriguing example. Conceived by Chinese real estate developer Zhang Xin, the Commune is a showcase of creative Asian talent: a collection of houses, all inspiringly and demonstrably different, and arranged together on a walled estate immediately adjacent to the Great Wall. Considering the prices of the houses – in the millions of dollars, unimaginable sums to ordinary Chinese – the name Commune is an ironic reference to the ideals expounded by Chairman Mao's *Little Red Book*. The Commune is beautiful and unique, but it also has that special twinkle of irreverence, mildly poking fun at China's inherited regime.

What's clear is that there's a consistency throughout, in sheer nerve and daring. Zhang could easily have followed the example of Beijing and trawled the high-profile names of international architecture for submissions. Yet it's just as well she didn't. The Chinese dream client, it turns out, has developed a monumental case of cold feet. All over Beijing, much-fanfared projects are being scrapped, and even those that are too far advanced to stop are being subjected to cost-cutting measures and enforced design changes. Pragmatism, a word hardly mentioned just a few years ago, is now the new Holy Grail. The problem, as it turns out, was one of miscommunication. Whenever China wants to be a world player in a new

arena, it sets out to hire the best talent to steer things in the right direction. The problem with architecture is that 'best' is a relative concept. Best may mean best known or famous – or it may mean best in utilitarian terms, i.e. a practice that gets a project in on time and below budget. The Chinese thought they were getting both. That was a misunderstanding that has involved billions of dollars. With a less dramatic scale and non-superstar architects, Zhang has chosen a purer path and in doing so has created one of the most compelling hotels in Asia.

The drive to the Great Wall takes under an hour from the centre of Beijing, but the total change in environment and ambience makes it feel like you've travelled for weeks, not minutes. Beijing is flat, dense, polluted and choked with traffic; the Great Wall snakes through a stretch of densely forested mountains punctuated by the odd clump of granite. There are no factories or office buildings, which for fast-growing China is rare. A small side road takes you past the Wall and winds into the mountains until you reach an avant-garde-designed metal gate. Beyond this starts the hotel–architecture park known as the Commune by the Great Wall. Twelve different villas designed by twelve different architects are scattered along the two-thousand-acre property, culminating in a large concrete and glass pavilion that houses two restaurants, three bars, a swimming pool and a reception lobby. The best words to describe this Commune are fearless and experimental; fearless in its willingness to take risks and experimental in openly embracing the new, in brazen defiance of convention. The clubhouse, for instance, has walls covered in peacock feathers, rabbit fur and tree bark, and organically shaped wash basins moulded in hammered copper. The emphasis, both architecturally and decoratively, is on being original. It represents innovation that verges on the fringe of art. That's why the Commune made its 2002 world debut at the Venice Biennale.

address Commune by the Great Wall, The Great Wall, Badaling Highway (Shuigan exit) 102102, China

t +86 (0)10 6567 3333 **f** +86 (0)10 6568 6313 **e** reservation@commune.com.cn

room rates from US$888

fuchun

Set in the verdant, uniquely Chinese landscape of Hangzhou, the traditional retreat destination of mainland China, Fuchun looks just like a Chinese watercolour. As it turns out, I wasn't the first to think so. The hotel is built on the exact location that inspired the legendary Yuan Dynasty painter Huang Gongwang to focus on a handscroll that took over ten years to complete. Although he didn't start painting until the age of fifty-one, Huang is credited with the reinvention of Chinese landscape painting. From the Tang to the Sung and then the Yuan Dynasties, painting in China was so grounded in tradition that it became stagnant. Huang was a revolutionary: bored of strictly imitating the masters, he began to paint what he *felt* rather than what he saw. Together with Ni Zan, Wu Zhen and Wang Meng, he became known as one of the Four Masters of the Yuan, regarded by some as China's first impressionists.

At the ripe old age of seventy-four, Huang moved to the Fuchun region and started work on *Dwelling in the Fuchun mountains*, the scroll that would seal his fame and many centuries later serve as inspiration for the extraordinary Fuchun Resort. Most days he would wander the mountains with his paper, brushes and ink, and paint still lifes of whatever inspired him. On his return home he would painstakingly transfer his creative efforts to the scroll. Finally, in the year he turned eighty-four, he finished his now famous painting.

It's a good story, worthy of a slow-moving, beautifully filmed Chinese movie, and one that caught the imagination of a driven Taiwanese industrialist. Bengo Cheng is a successful paper producer with factories all over mainland China as well as on the island of Taiwan. His success has allowed him to pursue his passions, one of which is traditional Chinese culture. He imagined a retreat that would celebrate rather than ignore Chinese history, and so he set about the ambitious project of Fuchun Resort. Stage one was a golf course, a clubhouse and some residential villas. Normally, at this point, my eyes would glaze over, not because I don't like golf but because I don't find golf courses very interesting. Fuchun, however, is the first place I've seen where the natural beauty of the surroundings is actually enhanced by a golf course, all entirely thanks to landscape design. The course's eighteen holes follow the contour of the land, while the clubhouse is built in Taoist style on an island in a spectacular manmade lake. But the creative *tour-de-force*

Set in the middle of a lake, the architecture and design of Fuchun is inspired by Taoist tradition.

Bedrooms are decorated in a modern take on 1920s Chinese Art Deco and arranged along elaborate courtyards.

Fuchun's landscape is straight out of a Chinese scroll painting; the terraces of a tea plantation adds a geometric edge.

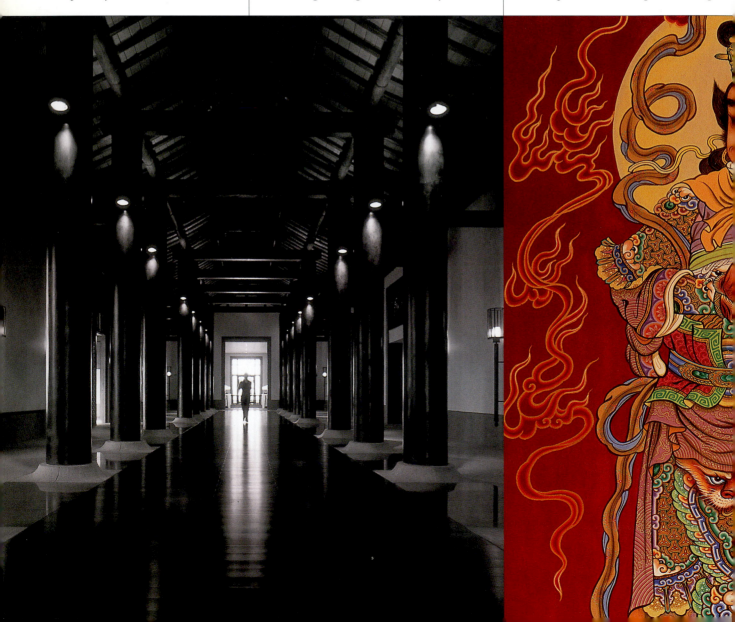

Fuchun is the result of
the proprietor's passion for
Chinese history and culture.

The lobby is an immense hall,
a virtual forest of towering
teak pillars.

Architecturally, the most inspiring space
is the soaring, temple-like structure that
houses the indoor swimming pool.

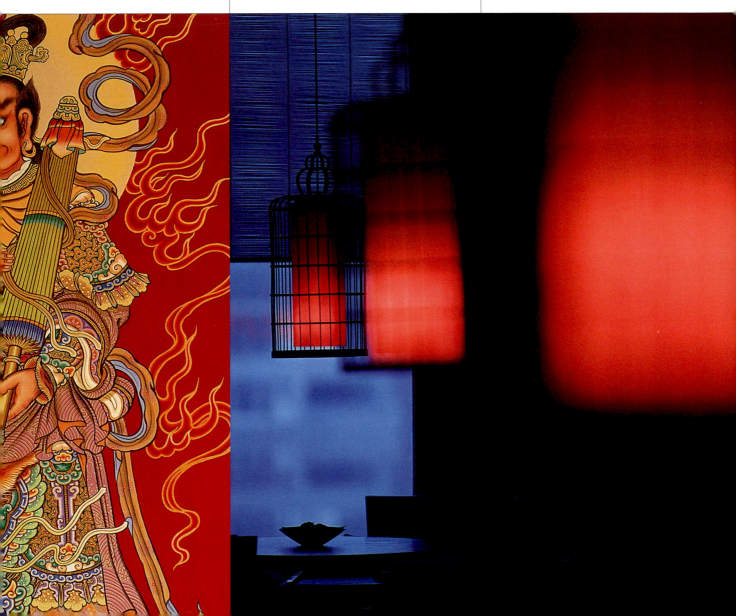

was the decision to surround the course with the boldly architectural terraces of a working tea plantation. In many places the tea grows all the way up to the fairway.

When the course and the clubhouse were completed in 2000, they caused quite a stir around the world. *Golf Digest* named Fuchun the best course in Asia, and *Condé Nast Traveller* voted T8, the club's restaurant, one of the fifty best in the world. Even Giorgio Armani came to see what all the fuss was about. It was one of those rare design success stories, a hit with locals and foreigners alike. But the best was still to come.

The hotel, which opened in October 2004, rises like a modern version of a Taoist temple in the middle of the lake opposite the clubhouse. With its traditional roof tiles and sloping walls of light grey granite, Fuchun has a distinctly Chinese aesthetic without being a pastiche of historical clichés. The same holds true for the interior. The granite floors, the China red carpet, the occasional strip of copper-coloured silk, the rows of massive columns and the bronze lanterns that line the corridors all pay tribute to the history of China and to the talent of Kuala Lumpur-based French architect Jean-Michel Gathy. And I haven't even mentioned the pool; you're not likely to find another one like it anywhere in the world. At over 250 square feet and entirely clad in copper- and gold-coloured mosaic glass tiles, it's located in a soaring structure defined by giant pillars and a typically Chinese interlocking beamed roof. If you can imagine swimming in a temple, then this comes close. And then there are the rooms. Arranged along a series of water gardens, they are vast apartments of oiled teak, copper silk, black stone and grey granite equipped to the highest standards of any Asian hotel (think Aman).

With a surrounding landscape straight out of a painting, the luxury of a princely palace, and the privacy and privilege only afforded to China's feudal warlords, Fuchun offers the China of myth − even if you don't play golf.

---

address Fuchun Resort, Hua Shu Village, Fuyang, Hangzhou, Zhejiang, China

t +86 (0)571 6346 1111 **f** +86 (0)571 6346 1222 **e** fuchunresort@lcpc.biz

room rates from US$250

adrère amellal

Before marching his troops eastwards to Persia, in 331 BC Alexander the Great made a little known detour to the distant oasis of Siwa. It had long been whispered that Alexander was the son of the god Amun, and he came to Siwa to consult the legendary Oracle of Amun and discover whether this was true. Though we'll never know exactly what happened there, it seems that Alexander left Siwa with the answer he was looking for. He returned from the desert to embark upon some of the greatest conquests in the history of civilization.

The most extraordinary thing about Siwa today is that the place is not so different from the time of the Macedonian conqueror's visit. Its inhabitants still speak a Berber language, Siwi, and their customs and traditions have changed little. Islam may have replaced animism as the mainstay of their beliefs, but the people's way of life remains the same: there's no industry, there are more donkeys than cars, and most of them still make a living from growing and selling dates and olives.

If you stay at Adrère Amellal, the impression that time has passed by this niche of the North African Sahara is even more pronounced. The architecture, decoration and building materials (salt, timber from palm trees and baked mud) are just as they would have been more than two thousand years ago. Add to this the fact that there are no telephones or electricity and the time warp is complete.

Adrère Amellal offers the most complete escape imaginable, not just from daily routine but from the world as we know it. Set beside an enormous saltwater lake, it's hard to believe that you're sixty feet below sea level, bang in the middle of the world's largest sand deposit. But, you may ask (as most people do), how comfortable is it to live without electricity or modern telecommunications? The answer, surprisingly perhaps, is that it's not only comfortable; it's actually quite luxurious. With the exception of being on a commercial flight, it's one of the few opportunities to exist without being telephoned, e-mailed or text-messaged. No one needs to be convinced of the romance of dining by candlelight, but the experience of a bedroom and bathroom illuminated solely by dozens of candles (all in natural beeswax) is something few of us have encountered. Suddenly your skin looks radiant and you can forget about make-up. In other words, it's conducive to total relaxation.

As an intelligent concession to the expectations of Western travellers, there are

bathrooms galore (with plenty of hot water and water pressure), but the real luxury of this hotel is not in the bathrooms or the bedrooms. It's in the experience. I defy anyone to come here and not return home with at least a handful of dinner party stories. Take, for instance, the lake: unlikely as it may be, your room is on the shore of a massive body of water that dominates the scenery in every direction. More unusual still, it is completely without water traffic. None. No boats, no fishing craft, not even the odd felucca so common on the Nile. This emptiness only adds to the spare machismo of the landscape. And then there's the unexpected plus that the lake is brilliant for swimming – or rather floating. With similar remedial properties to the Dead Sea, it's so salty that it's almost impossible to submerge.

And then there's the Sahara. Think of a celluloid fantasy set in the desert: *Laurence of Arabia*, *The Mummy*, *The Scorpion King*, *Beau Geste* or even the sci-fi film *Dune* – any of these could have been shot in the area around Siwa. It's a vast expanse of rippling dunes straight out of *The English Patient*. Even if you've been to countless other deserts (which I have), nothing can prepare you for what you'll encounter here. Alone and surrounded by endless mountains of talcum-powder-quality sand, a guide will take you on a 'Sahara rollercoaster', where you drive with tyres deflated at breathtaking speed. And just when you think you've seen it all, you hurtle down the side of yet another mammoth dune and find yourself at a different lake. You're free to dive straight into the water, which is surprisingly cold and deep. Swimming in the middle of the Sahara's sand dunes is an experience you're not likely to forget.

Appropriately enough, since we're less than thirty miles from the Libyan border, I remember seeing footage of Colonel Gadaffi disappearing on a regular basis to camp out in the desert. I'd never really understood what the fascination was. It wasn't something I could relate to…until Siwa.

address Adrère Amellal Oasis, Sidi al-Ja'afar, Siwa, Egypt

t +20 (0)2 738 1327 **f** +20 (0)2 735 5489 **e** info@eqi.com.eg

room rates from US$300

the old cataract

Long before his name became a brand, Thomas Cook was a real live person with a passion for Egypt. He wanted to share this passion, and in doing so became the world's first tour operator. Towards the end of the nineteenth century, a time when travel was not yet taken for granted, he was known, in certain circles, as the man who organized very successful tours of the Nile.

Cook's adventure tour of Egypt would start near Cairo with the pyramids of Giza. Next, the steamship would continue up to Luxor, where Cook's guests would visit the Valley of the Kings and stay at the rather grand Winter Palace (which, as its name suggests, was once the winter residence of the Egyptian royal family). Then it was back on board for the final leg of the journey to Aswan, site of the Nile's first cataract or waterfall, and source of the enormous granite blocks that distinguish ancient Egyptian architecture. Aswan was and is a particularly scenic part of the Nile. The river is at its broadest here, and is split by a series of emerald islands, the largest of which is Elephantine. Once upon a time, Aswan was the place where Egypt finished and Nubia (now Sudan) began; the carvings on the large stones that dip into the river attest to the ancient significance of this place as a gateway to the kingdom of the Pharaohs. It was therefore an appropriate climax to Cook's Egyptian tour. The only trouble was, there was nowhere for his illustrious clients to stay, and there was a limit to how long visitors could be expected to remain on board in the Egyptian heat, particularly in Victorian dress.

Thus in 1899 Thomas Cook built a hotel from scratch. On the outside, the rather grand pile was pure Victoriana – British colonial architecture at its culturally blindfolded best. Not a trace of Egyptian reference was to be found; it was a collection of windows, balconies and pillars that you could have found anywhere in the British empire. Inside, however, was a different story. Here was a vivid and eccentric collection of Eastern decorative signatures: an arabesque folly of Cordoba-style Moorish arches, polished stone floors, and lots and lots of *mashrabiya*, the intricate carvings on wooden screens widely used in Morocco and Egypt to provide privacy to one's harem. In the restaurant, today called 1902, the decorative stakes were raised a notch, recreating a fantasy version of a Moorish hall with soaring ceiling height, coloured glass and distinctive red and white arches. It's an overwhelmingly exotic space – exactly as it was intended.

From the day it opened, the Old Cataract was a hit, with its superb elevated location opposite Elephantine and its magnificent view over the Nile. Over the years its guestbook grew into a *Who's Who* of famous names, and eventually regulars such as Winston Churchill and Agatha Christie had suites named after them (though countless others, including the likes of Tsar Nicholas II, did not).

Up until the late 1950s, the Old Cataract was *the* place to stay in Aswan. But then the feistily independent President Gamal Abdel Nasser arrived on the scene. He drew up ambitious plans for Aswan's High Dam and, in a blatantly anti-Western move, awarded the contract to the Soviet Union. In 1963 the New Cataract Hotel was opened in an effort to accommodate the six hundred-odd engineers working on the project. Stylistically, the hotel was as independent and modern-minded as Nasser himself. A tall, imposing piece of mid-century modernism, its white, bright, clean-lined interiors were the architectural opposite of the Old Cataract's dusky grand corridors and velvet-upholstered mahogany furniture. The style of the New Cataract was 'groovy sixties' with a Pharaonic twist and it soon replaced the Old Cataract as Aswan's best place to stay. By the time French hospitality giant Accor stepped in, the Old Cataract had been empty and disused for almost a couple of decades. But the company had guessed that with the onset of mass tourism, people would want a return to the style, grace and charm of the Old Cataract. And they were right.

Today, the Old Cataract is once more the place to stay in Aswan. The renovation of the property has been sensitive and discreet: judging from old photographs, not much has changed. A lot of work has gone into installing all-new bathrooms, new plumbing and comprehensive air-conditioning, but not to the detriment of the hotel's colonial grandeur. Again, the world's leaders and celebrities feature heavily in the guestbooks. And Thomas Cook can rest in peace.

---

address Sofitel Old Cataract, Abtal El Tahrir Street, Aswan, Egypt

t +20 (0)97 316 000 **f** +20 (0)97 316 011 **e** H1666@accor-hotels.com

room rates from US$82

jia

In Mandarin, *jia* means home. The name is intended to be taken literally, as in the place where you live. Unlike most hotels in Hong Kong that cater predominantly to business travellers, Jia was designed for long-term residents. Even the smallest rooms are serviced apartments, complete with fully stocked kitchen, bathroom, living area, working space, separate sleeping area and generous storage. Anyone who spends time in hotels knows how rare it is to get anything without being billed for it, but Jia offers guests a multitude of extras at no additional charge; broadband is complimentary, as are phone calls, breakfast, the newspapers and a glass of wine when you arrive in the evening.

But the real triumph of Jia is the design by Philippe Starck. It's not so much the Starck signature, which in the world of hotels is not exactly groundbreaking, but rather the use of space. It's remarkable what Starck has been able to do with square footage that elsewhere would be put aside for a cupboard. Three hundred and eighty square feet is small by anyone's standards, and yet at Jia this is enough space for a studio. The white marble kitchen comes with a fridge, freezer, built-in microwave, stove top and sink. The spacious all-marble bathroom features a big, proper shower, a medicine cabinet hidden behind a mauve-coloured Venetian mirror, a lemon-coloured niche for towels and the engagingly attractive Starck signature washbowl on a marble table. The sitting area sports a slouchy white linen couch, a couple of coffee tables and a bunch of stools, while the sleeping space is defined by a floor-to-ceiling curtain. There's also plenty of storage, a large desk with its own filing drawers and built-in cupboards that hide domestic essentials such as an ironing board and hairdryer. Normally I don't describe a hotel room in such detail, but I've never come across space that has been so carefully and cleverly utilized. It's the kind of ingenuity that makes you rethink the possibilities of small spaces and gets you motivated to find a cubby hole of your own.

This design approach is particularly appropriate for Starck, who has a personal preference for cosy spaces. In step with his international profile, he has houses in Venice, Paris, New York and on the French Atlantic coast, and the thing they all have in common is their small size. Small is the way Starck chooses to live, and he's brought his particular way of thinking to the design of Jia's apartments.

It's Starck's international flair with work for companies as diverse as Japanese breweries, Italian furniture manufacturers, Dutch electronic giants and French mail-order houses that have made him famous, but it is this project in Hong Kong that reveals his previously unrecognized talent for addressing mundane needs in a competent, pragmatic fashion without sacrificing his sassy, cheeky modern aesthetic. Who else could combine a place reserved for an ironing board and a microwave with a silver plastic stool in the shape of a tooth?

Starck is also a businessman. Jia is a joint venture between his property development group Yoo and young Singaporean entrepreneur Yenn Wong's company PC Asia. Sure, there's a certain sense of formula to the design content, but there's no denying that Hong Kong needed a place like this. In the Asian world of black, gold and beige business hotels, Jia is the first to make an independent stand. Starck may not be new in town – he designed Felix bar and restaurant for the Peninsula – but it's certainly the first time an entire hotel here has been devoted to his particular brand of creativity.

Location-wise, Jia could not be more Hong Kong. Bang in the heart of Causeway Bay, the most concentrated shopping strip on the island, Jia is surrounded by more neon, more people and more frenetic bee-like activity than in the busiest street scene of a futuristic sci-fi film. You could satisfy the shopping appetite of a small European nation on one street alone. Nearby Times Square offers the world's largest collection of theme restaurants under one roof: if you want a swap from traditional Szechuan to fusion Japanese, for example, just take the escalator to the next floor.

Causeway Bay is an area not traditionally associated with hotels catering to foreign visitors, and that's exactly what makes it so much fun. And Jia gives you a real city pad in the thick of one of the world's most exciting cities.

address Jia Boutique Hotel, 1–5 Irving Street, Causeway Bay, Hong Kong
t +852 3196 9000 **f** +852 3196 9001 **e** info@jiahongkong.com
room rates from HK$995

aman-i-khás

The tiger is one of the most potent symbols in Asia. Revered for its strength, admired for its beauty and feared for its ability as a hunter, it features heavily in the region's artistic and cultural expression and appears on everything from Korean wall panels to Chinese silk and Indian murals. The trouble is, there aren't many tigers left.

A hundred years ago they were plentiful throughout Rajasthan, and the ruling princes were celebrated for the number of kills they tallied in a lifetime of passionate tiger-hunting. Hunting for the Rajputs was more than a sport; it was a lifestyle. An expedition could last several months: the maharaja would bring his ministers and advisers along so that matters of state could continue, hunting notwithstanding. And unimaginable as it may seem, he would spend weeks and weeks in a tent. But what a tent. This was a palace of cloth, with a banquet hall, separate chambers for matters of state, a private area for his wives and a rather grand bedroom. One such tent survives in the royal fort palace in Jodhpur: made of heavy red velvet and laboriously finished with stitching in real gold thread, it wouldn't exactly fit in a backpack, but nevertheless it's a dwelling that could be moved on a regular basis.

Considering the role both the tent and the tiger have played in Rajasthan's past, it's easy to understand why Aman launched its entry into India with a tiger camp in Ranthambore, India's best known tiger reserve. A three-hour drive from Jaipur, Ranthambore is how all of Rajasthan used to be: lush, low forest interrupted by patches of savanna-like bush, with stagnant green ponds and bare, rocky outcrops. In short, classic tiger country. Aman-i-Khás gives the visitor to India a chance to witness tigers on their own turf. Elsewhere in Rajasthan, there's not much chance of sighting one. Their natural habitat no longer exists – a casualty of extensive clearing for farming, chopping trees for firewood and the voracious appetites of goats and camels.

The reality of seeing a tiger in the wild lives up to all expectations. The manager, who's been at the camp since it opened, confessed to me that at first he wasn't much of a nature lover. But now he lives for the thrill of spotting one of these magnificent beasts. The tigers aren't a bit threatened by the sight of a car and happily go on doing what they do – which, apart from the occasional quest for food, involves lots of lazy lolling in the muddy waters of the countless nearby watering holes.

Like the Maharaja of Jodhpur's tent, Aman-i-Khás's 'rooms' are canvas palaces in their own right. Each guest tent is divided into several areas: a netted interior veranda; an entrance hall; a central lounge over twenty feet in height; a changing area with beautifully crafted teak cabinets and his-and-hers sinks; a separate bathroom with shower stall, sunken bath and toilet; another dressing area with hanging space for as much khaki as you could possibly need; and, finally, a rather spacious stateroom for sleeping in, complete with two desks and a trunk at the base of the bed, which disguises a handy guest fridge. On top of all this, the tent has air-conditioning and a central ceiling fan, as well as a plentiful supply of hot water.

Tent it may be, but you quickly grasp that this is roughing it maharaja-style. Fortunately, all these mod cons are ingeniously well hidden, so you get the fun of staying in a tent with the sophisticated chic of a modern Oriental interior. Still, 'camping out' is hardly an accurate description of the experience here. In typical Aman fashion, luxury and comfort are not sacrificed for the sake of adventure. One tent is equipped with a comprehensive spa that offers Rajasthani massage as well as Ayurvedic treatments, while another serves as a library. There's also a separate dining tent, and as might be expected, the food has little in common with the tin cans heated over a tiny gas pit of most people's camping experience.

As for the setting, Ranthambore is a magical place. At dusk, when the heat of the day shimmers languorously over the savanna and a fire is burning in the massive bronze urn that was once used for mixing enough *dahl* to feed an entire village during festivals, there's an ambience that is somehow evocative of the original Rajasthani tiger hunts. The combination of tents, open four-wheel drive and the promise of spotting tigers conjures up the adventure and romance of a real safari − minus the bullets and the discomfort.

address Aman-i-Khás, Ranthambhore, Rajasthan, India

t +91 (0)74 62 252 052 **f** +91 (0)74 62 252 178 **e** aman-i-khas@amanresorts.com

room rates from US$2,250 for three nights

devi garh

India's historical legacy is second to none. Few people realize that the culture of this vast subcontinent predates that of the Ancient Egyptians, or that the Indus Valley was home to the largest of the four ancient urban civilizations of India, Egypt, Mesopotamia and China. India was top on Alexander the Great's conquest list, and even the classical civilizations of the Mediterranean such as Greece and Rome coveted the region's beautiful silks.

It's because of all this history that India's architectural heritage is hard to match. In the northern state of Rajasthan, where the hot, dry weather has been particularly kind to buildings of substance, there is a wealth of awe-inspiring historical reminders of the fact that India was home to an aesthetically sophisticated culture long before the Brits arrived. Far ahead of Alexander the Great's ill-fated attempt to reach this fabled land of silk and tigers, Indian civilization invented the number system we now take for granted in mathematics (among many other contributions that seem to be forgotten, at least by the rest of the world).

As in France, India's many rulers (the subcontinent was divided into hundreds of tiny fiefdoms) built magnificent palaces, grand follies endowed with marble, stone and wood carving, inlaid jewels, fountains, gardens and even swimming pools in the form of stepwells (upside-down four-storey structures burrowed into the ground). Eventually the same fate befell India's aristocratic residences as the châteaux of France: the nobility could no longer afford to keep them. Following Independence in 1947, the country's former ruling classes had to find new ways of making ends meet, and one of the few options open to them was to convert their palatial properties into hotels. That's how Udaipur's fabulous Lake Palace came to be a hotel; the same goes for Jaipur's Rambagh Palace and many others. The trouble was, there weren't enough visitors to justify the restoration of India's myriad of (so-called) lesser palaces and forts. Or so everyone thought, until a small creative team with lots of zeal, plenty of imagination and the necessary financial means tackled the renovation of Neemrana Fort Palace near Delhi. Looking like a Rajasthani palace while feeling nothing like a hotel, Neemrana set a new benchmark. The response was immediate, and it's as hip today as it was when it first opened.

The success of Neemrana inspired a dream to renovate another Rajasthani palace.

Taking care to retain the original external architecture, the interior was to be reinvented in a style that could best be described as funky Indian minimalism: a traditional palace on the outside and a pared-down, monochromatic series of spaces on the inside. Nestled in the Aravali hills about an hour's drive from Udaipur, the eighteenth-century Devi Garh Fort Palace had been abandoned in the 1960s. By the time the Poddar family found it a couple of decades later it was a total wreck. Photographs taken at the start of the project reveal a ruin, an almost unrecognizable pile of rubble and stone – little wonder that it took over a decade to bring to fruition. Undeterred, Lekha Poddar's vision was of a soothingly spacious interior environment. With minimal decorative detail, Devi Garh was to be luxurious in a thoroughly contemporary yet unmistakably Indian manner.

The result is a model for all future historical projects in India. The palace is inspiringly beautiful, and the contrast between antique authenticity and minimalist modernity is nothing less than striking. What I couldn't help noticing, especially after having visited many other palaces, is how the hotel's reductivist approach amplifies its Indianness: the Mughal arches, the stone carving and all its other distinctive architectural signatures end up both clearer and stronger. In a sense, there's a parallel with the Taj Mahal. Up close this emblematic edifice is a highly ornate collection of niches, carvings and inlaid jewelry. From a distance, though, it's an immaculate fairytale structure, perfect in its whiteness. Its real visual strength lies not in its details but in the abstraction of its form.

With Devi Garh, the Poddars have struck just the right balance between a passion for history and a lust for contemporary luxury. Instead of relying on gold taps and fluffy towels, they have used sophisticated architecture and interior design to create a timeless blend of culture, history and space. It's a powerfully attractive combination.

address Devi Garh, Village Delwara, Tehsil Nathdwara, District Rajsamand, Rajasthan, India
t +91 (0)29 53 289 211 **f** +91 (0)29 53 289 357 **e** devigarh@deviresorts.com
room rates from US$150

umaid bhawan palace

Turbans, tigers and *White Mischief* in the Jazz Age. What fun India must have been in the Roaring Twenties: tiger hunts during the day, gin and tonics at night, doing the charleston at fancy dress galas in the magnificence of one of countless maharajas' palaces. For a lucky few, this was definitely not 'the land of heat and dust'.

In all the splendour of the Raj, no one was more legendary than Maharaja Umaid Singh of Jodhpur. The Maharaja's family, also known as the Rathore Rajputs, were the Indian Kennedys of their day: wealthy, educated, and tight with royals and movie stars alike, they were so good at polo that they invented the trousers for looking good while playing it. India has plenty of palaces, many of which have been converted into hotels – some more spectacularly than others – but nowhere comes close to Umaid Bhawan Palace, the Rathore Rajputs' family home in Jodhpur. It makes the White House look like a neoclassical cottage; even Buckingham Palace seems tiny by comparison. In fact, it's about the same size as Capitol Hill, and with its dominant position over Jodhpur's skyline, it could easily be mistaken for a seat of government.

How big is Umaid Bhawan? According to the family, the house is over two hundred thousand square feet, and the main hall, a stately rotunda, rises to a height of nearly two hundred feet. Along one flank of the perfectly symmetrical building resides the Maharaja's private four-carriage train, set on its own tracks. Underground, there's a vast mosaic pool that would not have looked out of place on the Titanic. In the garden, there are two squash courts – nothing special, you might say, except for the fact that they're made of marble – while back inside, you find no fewer than 347 rooms, hardly any of which resemble what you and I would normally call a 'room'. There are baronial halls panelled in dark timber, just like in a Scottish castle; a billiard room that makes serious business of shooting some pool; a cinema; a library; a fully fledged museum; and a double ballroom that could easily host the Ice Capades. There's a room for this and a room for that – it's hard to keep track. And throughout this monumental extravaganza, there's the most politically incorrect decoration imaginable. Tiger skins, elephant feet, buffalo horns, stuffed leopards; all the bounty of many decades of family hunts is proudly on display.

the tawaraya

Kyoto's Tawaraya is a national treasure: a supremely, sublimely Japanese *ryokan* (traditional inn) that has entertained household names such as Marlon Brando, James Michener, Leonard Bernstein, Jack Nicholson, Isaac Stern, Pierre Trudeau, Alfred Hitchcock, Richard Avedon, Jean-Paul Sartre, Peter Ustinov and Willem de Kooning, to list but a few.

Of the eighty thousand-odd ryokans spread around Japan, the Tawaraya is one of the oldest and definitely the most famous. Even though all the inn's components – the bamboo, the paper screens, the dark wood floors, the *tatami* mats, the cedar bathtubs and the precisely art-directed garden – are cultural staples, the exquisitely beautiful rooms somehow don't feel traditional in a backward-looking way. Instead, they feel modern and contemporary. The guest has the extremely rare privilege of experiencing an internal environment arranged entirely according to the guiding principles of *wabi*, the Zen notion of reducing something to the point where nothing further can be taken away. You live in a space where all that's left is sublimely simple perfection: not an empty room but a perfect space made up only of essentials (two very different things). It's the kind of environment

that makes you want to throw out the family silver and heirlooms when you get back home. True, the gardens are immaculate and the rooms are splendid in their refined Zen simplicity, but the Tawaraya experience is not just a visual one. It involves all the senses. For your ears, there's the silence: no muzak, no televisions in the background, no clatter of plates, no ding when elevator doors open, no electronic noises made by electronic doorlocks...there is an almost complete absence of noise. The only sound you hear is the soft swish made by the kimono-clad hostesses as they glide across the tatami and wood in their socks. For your tastebuds, there's the ten-course traditional *kaiseki* dinner served on a low table in your room. There is no dining room, restaurant, bar or breakfast nook at the Tawaraya; the emphasis is on total privacy and personal experience – like a monk, albeit a spoiled one. And for your feet, there's the smooth transition of textures as the floors change from tatami to polished wood to bamboo and back again in a tactile rhythm dedicated to your bare foot.

Beauty, simplicity, silence, texture, taste, tradition – these are the key words of the Tawaraya experience. And yet they are terribly inadequate. They mention nothing, for instance, of the legendary level of service – the kind of service that happens all by itself, that relies on anticipation and intuition, not suggestion or command. The *nakai* (ryokan staff) don't speak fluent English, which is wonderful – what they say and how they say it fits perfectly with the experience (what a pity it would be if someone suddenly blurted out, 'Have a nice day'). Perhaps the most revealing testimonial comes from Baron Hilton himself, who described the Tawaraya as 'a lesson to hotel men on what service is all about'.

Admittedly, the Okazaki family has had a long time to get it right. The founding of the inn originally goes back to the first decade of the eighteenth century by Wasuke Okazaki, a successful textile merchant from the county of Tawara. He sent his son to open a trading post in Kyoto which also took in travelling merchants. Word spread that the Tawaraya was a comfortable and familiar place to stay in what was then the slightly forbidding imperial city.

The establishment slowly gained a reputation, and by 1904 the Tawaraya had been singled out in a guidebook to Kyoto as the best and most distinguished inn in town.

Today, Mrs Toshi Okazaki Satow is the eleventh generation of Okazakis to operate this historic inn, and she is evidently not one to rest on her ancestral laurels. Widow to the late Ernest Satow, a half-American professor of fine art at Kyoto City University of Arts and accomplished photographer in his own right, Mrs Satow continues to update and refine the interiors – not because the Tawaraya needs it, but because of a personal conviction that the inn must remain vibrant and contemporary.

And therein lies perhaps the most telling message of this enchanting ryokan: it's not a case of transporting the guest back into Japanese history but more one of bringing Japan's past into a contemporary context. It's inspiring to see age-old tradition translated into modern experience. The Tawaraya may be small, but its message is big.

address Tawaraya, Anenokoji-agaru, Fuya-cho, Nakagyo-ku, Kyoto 604-8094, Japan

t +81 (0)75 211 5566 **f** +85 (0)75 211 2204

room rates from Yen 35,000

three sisters inn

I'd come to Kyoto, old Kyoto, to experience a bit of Japanese authenticity: to eat in a noodle bar with taxi drivers and spend the night in a traditional Japanese inn – preferably one with an aesthetic of paper screens, wooden floors and straw tatami mats. It's a place where you sleep on a futon, where you eat on the floor with your legs crossed and your knees bang against a low lacquered table. All of which begs the question: why submit to what is essentially a disorienting experience, when even the Japanese themselves opted for Western-style beds and tables long ago?

The answer is because it's a chance to experience something different. Most people would be disappointed, for instance, to discover how little Japan resembles the land of *The Last Samurai*. As one of the most densely populated places on earth, Japan on the surface seems like urban clutter from one prefecture to the next. In the train from Osaka to Kyoto you see no countryside at all, just buildings and more buildings. Unlike in Europe where there is normally some discernible trace of a unifying style, here there is none – you have the impression that people build whatever, wherever. Yet the culture depicted in countless films still exists in many less obvious aspects of

day-to-day life. Zen is still very much alive in contemporary Japan. You can see it in the meticulous preparation and presentation of sushi; in the takeaway *bento* boxes so beautifully arranged and packaged that they're more like an anniversary present than a snack to be eaten on the train; in the spotless white gloves of the policemen; and in the linen and lace seat-covers in the taxis.

For the visitor to Japan, a stay at a ryokan is a must, and the Three Sisters Inn is one of the most enduring, charming and affordable of those that still exist in the former imperial city of Kyoto. It is also, without a doubt, the best located. Situated a stone's throw from two of Kyoto's most important monuments, the Kuradani Temple and the Heian Shrine, the inn is hidden in an idyllic residential part of the city, away from the bustle of downtown Kyoto. In fact, at night it's so devastatingly quiet that you can hear the traffic lights change from red to green from a block away.

The house that now operates as Three Sisters has been in the Yamada sisters' family for fourteen generations. Since 1957, Kikue, Sadako and Terumi (also known as Kay, Sandy and Terry) Yamada have been running their ancestral family home as an inn – and have

become famous for doing so. It's hard to find a guidebook that doesn't give them a glowing testimonial, and the walls of the reception are decorated with photos of the sisters with such luminaries as Senator Ted Kennedy, among others. All the thank-you letters are consistent: in essence, 'Thank you for the experience'. And just what is that experience? It's a personal glimpse into Japanese culture. No matter how many things you see, museums you go to, shrines you visit or books you read, nothing will give you the insight that one night at a ryokan will provide. Your room looks as if the ceiling has been lowered and the furniture has been removed, and one glance at the thin futon on the floor of your room and at first you're convinced that you'll never get a good night's sleep. Yet after one night, as most guests will confirm, you'll have slept better than you can remember. What's more, the clarity and precision of the space makes a normal hotel room seem clumsy and cluttered. A guestroom at Three Sisters is

a carefully considered box, executed only in natural materials such as wood, paper and tatami. It doesn't matter that there's no phone; in fact, I wished there had been no television.

Three Sisters is a perfect platform from which to explore Kyoto. It establishes a link between you and the city's past by accommodating you in its history. I've seldom been in a place where the guests have been on such on a mission to explore. Some were intent on shopping for antiques; others were researching textile traditions; others had a shopping list of temples to visit. But the common ingredient was a passion for Kyoto's treasures – a passion amplified by staying in this ryokan.

The sisters who run this unique inn are certainly old Japan. They belong to an era of kimonos and deep bows, but their Western training and impeccable English are there to soothe Western nerves, especially when it comes to scary things such as getting a taxi.

address The Three Sisters, Main Inn, Okazaki, Sakyo-ku, Kyoto 606-8321, Japan

t +81 (0)75 761 6336 **f** +81 (0)75 761 6338

room rates from Yen 13,000

alila

In Sanskrit, 'alila' means surprise – and this uptown Jakarta hotel is certainly that, in more ways than one.

The first surprise is the location: it's not at all what you'd expect from such an imposing piece of modern architecture. Whereas most of Jakarta's modern glass towers are situated around Lapangan Merdeka (Freedom Square) near Sudirman-Thamrin Road, Jakarta's main thoroughfare which is permanently clogged with traffic, Alila is on its own in what used to be known as the *bovenstad*, the city's centre of government during Dutch rule. Jakarta's handsome colonial buildings are just around the corner from here, as is another longstanding element of the city: Chinatown. Even before the arrival of the Dutch in 1596, this strategic port welcomed visitors from China, India, Malaysia, Siam and Japan, who would come to this harbour-town on the Java Sea to purchase gold, rhino horn and, of course, spices. Chinatown was a hub for trade, and today Alila stands bang in the middle it.

Jakartans think it's a strange location for a sleek, twenty-three-storey hotel, but after spending an exhausting, blisteringly hot day in Jakarta's traffic, the strategy behind Alila's positioning reveals itself to be not so strange at all. Although the Balinese describe Jakarta as Indonesia's Tokyo, it actually has more in common with Mexico City. Like its Central American counterpart, Jakarta is daunting in its vastness. Viewing it from the top floor of Alila, it's impossible to see where the city ends: it's a relentlessly sprawling metropolis of low-rise dwellings, shops and shacks, interrupted only by the odd cluster of high-rise glass towers. Walking, unfortunately, is not an option. But Alila's advantage is that, being in the colonial part of the city, it is far closer to the airport and slightly removed from the heaving congestion of Sudirman-Tharmin Road.

As in other megacities like São Paulo, locals seem to take the place's shortcomings in their stride. They may complain about the traffic, but they also take advantage of the opportunities: those in the know will tell you about Jakarta's fantastic restaurants, which cover virtually every cuisine imaginable. The point about Jakarta is that it doesn't really matter where you're located because the sybaritic advantages of this metropolis are always driving distance away. Alila may not be in the most *chichi* area, but this will make little difference in terms of your enjoyment of Indonesia's capital.

Surprisingly contemporary, Alila was designed by pioneering Aussie architectural firm DCM.

Subtle references to Alila's location in the Indonesian capital of Jakarta are found in its art and detail.

In the lobby a towering wall features an installation by artist Pieter Dietmar.

Modern art, strategically placed,
enhances the quality of the
outdoor spaces.

The pool bar on Alila's rooftop offers
privacy and space in the midst of a
dense urban centre.

Horizontal planes intersected by vertical
ones is the DCM signature that extends
to all the spaces in the hotel.

alila

This brings us to Alila's second surprise: Jakarta is not the city where I would have expected the avant-garde design boys from Melbourne to pop up. Anyone familiar with the work of John Denton, Bill Corker and Barrie Marshall (of the DCM Group) would know that they've made a name for staying ahead of the trend curve. And also how resistant they are to compromise. As a practice, DCM was working in Beijing before most designers had even considered venturing into China, and it was the first leading architectural firm to open an office behind the former Iron Curtain in Warsaw. Then you take into account Marshall's radical all-black beach house on Victoria's Phillip Island and you start to understand that DCM is an adventurous choice for any city property.

With Alila, DCM has struck exactly the right balance between a big, efficient business hotel with the latest communications gizmos, and a contemporary hangout that reflects Jakarta's emerging cosmopolitanism. For me, there was just one puzzling thing about its design: an elaborate concrete ramp leading to the hotel's elevated first-floor reception. It looked decidedly un-DCM, but no one I asked seemed to know any better. It wasn't until I was winding past the volcanoes of Central Java a few days later that my questions were answered. I mentioned where I'd been staying to the driver, and he blurted out, 'I know that hotel – it used to be a car showroom.' It was yet another surprise about Alila, and it made the choice of its architects seem even more inspired: converting a combination car showroom and boring office block into a street-smart, cutting-edge watering hole is not the simplest of tasks, but it was done so convincingly that if it hadn't been for a chance encounter with the volcano driver, it would have remained a metropolitan mystery.

I like the fact that Alila is in the wrong place – it gives the hotel some personality. And I really like the fact that it used to be a car showroom. Urban environments can definitely do with the element of surprise.

address Alila Jakarta, Jalan Pecenongan Kav. 7–17, Jakarta 10120, Indonesia
t +62 (0)21 231 6008 **f** +62 (0)21 231 6007 **e** jakarta@alilahotels.com
room rates from US$160

amanjiwo

It's difficult to convey the experience of staying at Amanjiwo. Sure, it's luxurious: many guest bungalows have their own swimming pool. It's also undeniably beautiful with its circular, temple-like forms that mimic the stupas of Borobudur, the monumental Buddhist sanctuary nearby. And then there are the silverleaf ceilings, the copper tabourets, the teak furniture and the blue-and-white batik cushions scattered along the sandstone steps of the restaurant; not to mention the immaculately dressed staff or the idyllic location, perched as it is against a dramatic hillside that looks like a Chinese watercolour landscape. But these are all tangible qualities, and it's the intangibles that make it so unique. There's a subtle mysticism to Amanjiwo: at the risk of sounding New Age, the place has a powerful spiritual energy.

One thing is certain: there's a link between Amanjiwo and Borobudur, and it's not just that they share visual consistencies. Borobudur is, after all, 'the mountain of a thousand statues', one of the most important archaeological and religious sites in Asia. Yet if it hadn't been for the curiosity of Thomas Stamford Raffles, governor general of Java (1811–1816), it might never have been found. Erected in around AD 800, Borobudur was largely forgotten on the island by 1700: most people had converted to Islam, and the remains of an abandoned religion hardly merited attention. But Raffles was fascinated by Asia's antique cultures and made it known that he was interested in any artifacts of Hindu or Buddhist provenance. Imagine his surprise when, in 1814, a villager handing over some bronze figurines mentioned that he knew of a vast but long-abandoned ruin that might be of interest. Intrigued, Raffles dispatched Dutch engineer H.C. Cornelius to investigate the site. Located deep within the island's interior, it had been so long neglected that it took two hundred men six weeks just to cut away the surrounding jungle.

But what they found was worth it. Predating Henri Mouhot's 'discovery' of Angkor in Cambodia by forty-six years, Borobudur's rediscovery opened Western eyes to the level of sophistication achieved by Southeast Asian civilizations. While it was a shock to witness the extent to which India's spiritual teachings had travelled, even more surprising was the fact that the world's largest and most magnificent Buddhist structure had been built on a remote island three thousand miles from India, rather than at the birthplace of Siddharta Gautama (Buddha) at the foot of the Himalayas.

Ironically, Borobudur tells us far more about the ancient Javanese than Javanese history can tell us about Borobudur. Without any kind of documentary records, which would have been kept on perishable material such as dried palm fronds, all theories concerning this monumental structure and the culture behind it are derived from its architecture. From the size of Borobudur, for instance, we know for certain that the Javanese had not only skilled craftsmen, but plenty of them. On this basis, historians suggest that many farmers in ancient Java were also part-time artisans, as they are in Bali today. From the number of stones (more than a million blocks weighing over two hundred pounds each) and the amount of carving (over five hundred lifesize statues and 1,460 bas-reliefs) at Borobudur, construction is estimated to have taken seventy-odd years, assuming that almost none of the workers would have been able to work full-time.

The history of Borobudur is fascinating and complex, full of unsolved mysteries. But when all's said and done, compelling as it is, Borobudur is a relic of a lost culture. Amanjiwo brings it back to life. Architect Ed Tuttle has sensitively managed to distill the style of the temple in the design of the hotel. The construction of the stone screens leading to the massive circular dining room, the columns supporting the roof and the form of the central building – all of these evoke the distinctive shapes and details of the nearby monument. But the connection is deeper than that. Thanks to clever planning, Amanjiwo functions as an observatory: everywhere you look from the hotel, the vista ends with Borobudur. The temple is omnipresent; it's no accident that the entire orientation of the hotel hinges on the view of the mountain of a thousand statues.

As Amanjiwo's staff move silently around the stone buildings preparing guestrooms for the night, so do their saffron-clad counterparts attend to the statues in the Buddhist sanctuary across the valley. It's the closest you'll ever get to sleeping in a temple.

---

address Amanjiwo, Borobudur, Central Java, Indonesia

t +62 (0)293 788 333   **f** +62 (0)293 788 355   **e** amanjiwo@amanresorts.com

room rates from US$650

Iosari coffee plantation

Java was once synonymous with coffee. The story of how Indonesia's most populated island became inextricably intertwined with the history of coffee is a fascinating tale.

It starts in the Middle East, where an imam is said to have noticed the hyperactivity of goats after they had grazed on a certain kind of berry. He used the berry to concoct a brew and found that it helped him to stay awake and even improved his ability to concentrate on his prayers. The word spread, and coffee (from the Arabic word *kaffe*) became as sought-after as spices. For many years it was cultivated only in Yemen, and the port of Mocha enjoyed a monopoly on the trade of coffee beans. In order to protect that monopoly, the export of their seedlings was made a crime punishable by death. Nevertheless, in the eighteenth century an enterprising young agent of the Dutch East India Company smuggled some of the celebrated plants to Holland, where they were handed over to Amsterdam's botanical gardens and cultivated in secrecy by scientists including the Swedish botanist Carl Linnaeus. They then sent their newly grown saplings to the Dutch East Indies for suitability tests. Java in particular, with its wet, steamy weather and high volcanic slopes, offered ideal conditions for growing the bean. Soon the plantations of Java could barely keep up with demand. Holland had caught the entire world by surprise, including the hapless merchants of Mocha. Within the space of fifty years, Java became the dominant source of the now heavily traded commodity, and until the late 1800s the quality of Java's *arabica* coffee beans was unsurpassed.

It's likely that Java would still dominate the world's coffee production today if it hadn't been for a catastrophe in the late nineteenth century: in a matter of months, nearly all of the island's arabica coffee crops were wiped out by a fungus called rust disease − only plants growing above an altitude of three thousand feet were unaffected. Word of the devastating blight got out, as did the more useful information about altitude resistance. Two nations in South America, Brazil and Colombia, had plenty of heat, rain and suitably elevated terrain, and this was the opening they had been looking for. Although the Dutch eventually managed to develop a new fungus-resistant variety called *robusta*, Java's dominance over the finer arabica bean was lost. Eventually the robusta beans would reach the prices of arabica, but by then South America had stolen Java's thunder.

In light of all this drama and intrigue, I was attracted to the notion of staying at a coffee plantation-turned-hotel on Java. Nestled among the volcanoes in the island's central highlands, Losari Coffee Plantation still produces some twenty tons of coffee beans a year, and its customers include famous brands such as Illy and Lavazza. Thus it continues to do what it's been doing since 1922, when a young Dutchman called Van der Swan took a lease on some beautiful but remote land high in the mountains of Java and called it Karangredjo. After Indonesia gained independence from the Netherlands in 1949, most plantations were nationalized, but Van der Swan was able to hold on to his estate along with its splendid Dutch colonial house. He eventually sold it to an Indonesian army colonel who kept it running until Gabriella Teggia chanced upon the property in 1991. A native of Rome who first came to Indonesia in 1965 and never left, Teggia was looking for property in Central Java when she stumbled across the Karangredjo plantation while out trekking. Together with some investors she purchased it and immediately changed its name to Losari after the village nearby.

Teggia's idea was to create a place where time would stand still, where the only reference to the outside world would be the plantation itself. In step with the emerging trend in Hip Hotels, Losari was designed to be an experience – in this case of a working coffee plantation. But that doesn't mean any sacrifices in terms of comfort. The old plantation house is now the library and living room, the bar resides in one of the old warehouses and guests stay in private villas dotted around the estate. There are also two restaurants, an octagonal swimming pool and a comprehensive spa.

When you lie in a hammock suspended between two of Losari's neoclassical pillars you can contemplate the incredible story of coffee. Who would have thought that such a little bean had such a big history?

---

address Desa Losari Grabag, P.O. Box 108, Magelang 56100, Central Java, Indonesia
t +62 (0)298 596 333 **f** +62 (0)298 592 696 **e** info@losaricoffeeplantation.com
room rates from US$250

muang kulaypan

In the ancient city of Muang Kulaypan in Java, there lived a prince called Inao Panyee Karatapati, whose reputation as a great lover and valiant warrior was as impressive as his name. The story of his romance with the beautiful Princess Budsaba travelled from Java to Thailand and it inspired a dance that was a favourite at the Thai royal court. Designer and decorator M.L. Archava Varavana is a member of Thailand's royal family, and his great-great-grandmother Chaochom Mandakhian was famous for playing the role of Inao in the Thai dance–drama (in Thai court dance, all roles are performed by women). When Varavana was asked to design a resort on Chaweng Beach on Koh Samui, a remote island in southern Thailand, he remembered that the legend of Prince Inao is thought to have taken place in this region, and so the name of Muang Kulaypan came to mind.

It's clear that Varavana takes his personal link to the heritage of Thailand very seriously, but it didn't stop him from applying an uncompromisingly modern approach to the architecture, design and decoration of Muang Kulaypan. Considering the hotel was designed in 1991, it would have been way ahead of its time anywhere in the world, let alone on this tiny island. With its Japanese-style bedrooms, teak floors, concrete walkways, sexy black-tiled bathrooms, black swimming pool and tie-dyed Marimekko bedspreads, the place is like a Danish modernist's dream of an upmarket Oriental beach shack.

How, I wondered, did the owner manage to convince this aristo-Thai to design such an unexpectedly avant-garde bolthole not far from where the movie *The Beach* was filmed? Although a hotel in this location was bound to be a sound investment, it doesn't explain the aesthetic discipline evident throughout, which bears no relation to the Koh Samui norm. The town adjacent to Chaweng Beach is filled to the rim with shops, restaurants, raunchy bars and rowdy discos. During the day, people chill out on the beautiful beaches; at night, they walk into town to party. It's a fun scene, but hardly the automatic choice for such an original and sophisticated hangout.

Stranger still is the fact that half the guests here seemed to be from France. The French are astute judges of value, so it makes sense that this hotel should appeal to French sensibilities. After all, it has a great Thai restaurant, Budsaba, where guests eat in the exquisite privacy of their own *sala* (a raised hut with low tables

and cushions); it dominates a sizeable slice of Chaweng Beach; design-wise the rooms are a cross between chic and Zen; staff are elegantly discreet; and prices are amazingly affordable. Even so, the hotel wasn't intended solely for one visiting nationality. The mystery of the hotel's French connection was solved when I met the proprietor of Muang Kulaypan, who speaks fluent French. It turns out that this stylish, distinguished Thai gentleman studied at the famous Ecole des Beaux-Arts in Paris, and so did his good friend Varavana. *Pas mal.*

Muang Kulaypan gets better the longer you stay. At first, impressions are purely visual, but there's an ambience of graciousness here that reveals itself more slowly. It's because the owner treats everyone as extended family. His staff, for instance, are provided with accommodation, meals, uniforms and health care. To use a phrase appropriate to the region, it's the kind of attitude that generates good karma. And then there's the hotel's naughty resident elephant Dunah, a happy, chubby little fella who gets into all sorts of mischief around the property. A year ago he was a mistreated, skinny orphan on the streets of Bangkok; now he's the darling of all the guests, and his daily swim is an event eagerly looked forward to.

Sensitivity is a quality that the owner and architect have applied to virtually everything at the hotel. On some evenings Budsaba features traditional Thai royal dance. Normally, when guest entertainment is announced, I run as fast as I can in the other direction; but the fact that you're invited to watch from the privacy (and safety from audience participation) of your sala makes all the difference. The dance, a mesmerizing display of costume and movement, is as seductive as the setting. Shimmering coloured silks, tall, elaborate architecture, fanciful dance in extraordinary costumes...what a deliciously exotic spectacle the kingdom of Siam must have been for its first foreign visitors. And you don't have to be French to appreciate how spectacular Thailand can be even today.

---

address Muang Kulaypan Hotel, 100 Moo2 Chaweng Beach, Koh Samui, Suratthani 84320, Thailand
t +66 (0)77 230036 **f** +66 (0)77 230031 **e** reservations@kulaypan.com
room rates from Baht 2,100

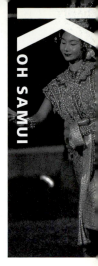

sila six senses

When you arrive at the newly completed Sila Six Senses complex on the Thai island of Koh Samui, the view is at once exhilarating and strangely familiar. The sweeping vista of palm-clustered islands and shimmering seas brings to mind all the fantasies we have of the Orient's beaches. This is appropriate because it's where part of the film *The Beach* (based on the book by Alex Garland) was shot.

The resort is made up of a stunning collection of bamboo-clad villas, all with their own infinity-edge swimming pool looking out over the Andaman Sea below. The place is almost universal in its appeal, an ideal version of what we would hope to find in the steamy tropics. This is about as far away from backpacking in Thailand as you can get. Together with Amanpuri in Phuket and the Four Seasons in Bangkok, Sila is one of the most expensive hotel properties in the old kingdom of Siam. But price is not the point, so much as what you get for your money. In Koh Samui, Sila gives you a lot, including a comprehensive spa that offers every conceivable treatment in Asia…with a brilliant view to boot.

The Six Senses brand is the creation of husband-and-wife team Sonu and Eva Shivdasani. They launched their vision of what a resort should be with Soneva Fushi in the Maldives almost a decade ago and haven't looked back since. In a world where hotel and resort companies are scrambling to be noticed, they have made their name by not second-guessing the consumer. By their own candid admission, they create places completely according to their own ideas of luxury and excellence. Eva, who was a model and fashion entrepreneur in Paris before meeting Sonu at the Monaco Grand Prix (where else?), describes their approach as analogous to a dinner table in a Louis XVI château: the linen and silver are replaced by coconut wood plates and hand-beaten bronze knives and forks, and the priceless Aubusson rug is substituted by even more precious barefoot toes in the sand. She has a point – a noble savage is more difficult to conjure than a consmopolitan dandy.

Six Senses is the embodiment of a new kind of hotel. The focus is on space, privacy and personal indulgence. At Sila there are no rooms as such, only villas. Each guest gets their own house with a private swimming pool, a modern interpretation of a traditional Thai residence, with open-plan, polished wooden

The use of bamboo in the visual architecture sets this place apart; it's like nothing else on Koh Samui.

Timber louvres, open-plan spaces and organically shaped lamps distinguish Sila's bathrooms.

Situated on the least developed, northernmost tip of the island, Sila is Koh Samui without the hubbub.

Each guest villa offers a loft-style layout with the added indulgence of a twenty-foot private swimming pool.

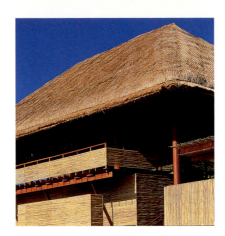

The public spaces are housed in open pavilions with unimpeded views of the shimmering seas below.

An open-plan space with a sunken tub, the villas' bathrooms are the size of most hotel rooms.

floors, louvres to filter light, subtly different levels that don't vary by more than a few steps and open-air spaces combined with a loft-like arrangement for the interior, i.e. no doors between the bedroom and bathroom. The restaurant and bar are open pavilions without air-conditioning or any form of glazing, deriving their aesthetic from the communal longhouses of traditional river communities. The view, the architecture, the decor, the style and even the temperature intentionally immerse the guest in the location.

The other distinguishing feature of this new style of hotel is the lifestyle. Today's savvy travellers no longer spend their days nursing a cocktail in a tacky half-submerged pool bar but split their time between exploring and being pampered. Hence, the Shivdasanis' philosophy behind their Six Senses resort is to endeavour to send their guests home glowing. The idea is fuelled by an emerging trend in tourism known as 'captive pampering': guests are cocooned in their secluded setting

with neither the means (i.e. transport) nor the motivation to leave. That's not to say you can't go out at night, but it's not that convenient because Sila is miles away from the nearest town or bar. And no one here is complaining. The aim of couples who arrive at this hideaway is to chill out and regenerate. They alternate between long, languorous meals, treatments at the spa and swimming in the private pools of their hillside villas. The only thing they're missing is the hustle and bustle of Chaweng Beach – but there, for many visitors to Koh Samui, once is often enough.

In many ways, Sila is following a well-established trend in Phuket of resorts moving further and further away from town in order to offer guests their own slice of beach Nirvana. Indeed, Sila is so well hidden on Samui that you would never stumble across it unless someone gave you specific directions. This is back to nature – without even a hint of roughing it.

address Sila Evason Hideaway, 9/10 Moo 5 Baan Plai Laem Borphut, Koh Samui, Suratthani 84320, Thailand

t +66 (0)77 245678   **f** +66 (0)77 245671   **e** reservations-samui@evasonhideaways.com

room rates from Baht 13,370

costa lanta

Koh Lanta is a different slice of Thailand. Located a few hours' drive south of the resort town of Krabi, its two islands of Lanta Noi (the smaller one) and Lanta Yai are a peaceful alternative to the flashier, better known Thai beach destinations of Koh Samui or Phuket. It takes two ferries and two dirt roads to get here. There's no nearby airport, no designer Italian restaurants on the beach, no busy shopping streets and absolutely no nightlife… unless you count geckoes and mosquitoes.

Until relatively recently, Koh Lanta was a thoroughly undiscovered part of Thailand. Five years ago, the island had no electricity and no telecommunications, and to this day there is an unhurried, agrarian pace of life. It was exactly this pristine wildness that attracted the family of Kasma Kantavanich who would holiday here when she was growing up, before it became known as the new Hua Hin or Phuket. Enchanted by the area's natural forest, sandy beaches, exceptional diving and signature clumps of rock sticking into the Andaman Sea, they even bought their own piece of bush on the beach on the northwestern edge of Lanta Yai. It was a purchase based on emotional impulse more than logical reasoning. They had no idea at

the time what to do with it, and for many years the family would simply go there and camp out. Then in 2000 everything changed. All of a sudden the area had electricity, telecommunications and…hotels. Lanta Yai had been 'discovered'. Kasma and her family were at a crossroads. What were they to do? Should they sell the land and look for an unspoilt Eden somewhere else? Or should they join in with the local development steadily gaining momentum? Though the arrival of tourists marked the end of an era, it was bound to provide a much-needed source of income and employment for the area. At least in opting to develop their own land, they would also be able to have an influence on the direction that tourism would take.

Thus, without any previous experience in the hotel industry, Kasma dived in. She assembled a group of investors and took on board Thai architect Duangrit Bunnag to tackle the question of aesthetics. Bunnag was full of ideas from his first visit, and according to Kasma he was already sketching schemes for the property on his flight back to Bangkok. At first no particular design approach was ruled out, including traditional architecture featuring peaked roofs and lots of gilding. Ultimately,

though, it was agreed to proceed in a modern, open direction.

Design-wise, it's a triumph of the box – the concrete box. Costa Lanta is not a hotel in the conventional sense. There are no rooms as such, only a collection of stand-alone houses arranged along a natural forest immediately behind the beach. The trees were the only inflexible part of the design brief, and the architect has used them as a way of providing each box with maximum privacy. The concrete bungalows are connected by a wooden walkway that snakes its way through the property and eventually ends at the dining bar and living pavilion located on the beach. As a design statement, it's both inventively original and pragmatically clever. The best view and location are reserved for the space that you're likely to spend the most time in: the dining and living area, which also happens to be the place closest to the water.

Ironically, the concrete box is more authentically Thai than you might expect.

The fact is that, throughout contemporary Asia, whether it's Cambodia, Malaysia, Myanmar or Indonesia, the simple concrete box is the people's choice. Some will lament the gradual extinction of traditional forms and shapes, but convenience, comfort and efficiency have overtaken convention and formality.

That said, the boxes at Costa Lanta are particularly comfortable and well designed. Divided into a sleeping area and a bathroom space, the box can be as open or as enclosed as you like: two of the four walls fold out completely, so during the day your box is open and at night it's closed. The bathroom, a monastic expanse of polished concrete, is surprisingly spacious with a smart translucent canopy-roof that floats above the walls, eliminating the need for extractor fans. The sleeping part is a box within a box within a box (a mosquito net enclosure inside the sleeping room box inside the outer concrete box). What you get is lifesize Russian doll architecture with a Thai twist.

address Costa Lanta, 212 Moo 1, Saladan, Amphur Koh Lanta, Krabi Province, Thailand

t +66 (0)2 660 3550 **f** +66 (0)2 260 9067 **e** info@costalanta.com

room rates from Baht 2,750

the apsara

Luang Prabang was a mystery to me. I knew next to nothing about Laos, and even less about this historic town on the mighty Mekong River. It was curiosity that compelled me to get on the flight from Bangkok. There was a daily flight to Luang Prabang, which meant that there must be enough people wanting to go to northern Laos to justify the frequency. Why, I wondered, are all these people going to this exotic-sounding destination, and what do they do when they get there?

The answer, I discovered, is quite straightforward: the attraction of Luang Prabang is the town itself. Protected in its entirety by a UNESCO heritage listing since 1995, it is exactly how one might imagine the traveller's fantasy of a perfect town in the tropics of the Far East, an exemplary piece of unspoilt Southeast Asia. Ten years ago, it had no electricity, running water or roads to speak of. It had been abandoned by the government, left to its own devices to crumble away slowly as a decaying symbol of the previous regime. But Luang Prabang was too important to ignore for long. After all, this had been the traditional seat of Laos's royal family; they had their palaces here and there were more temples than houses. What's more, when

the French became the resident colonial power, they built many impressive villas, most of which have survived intact because they were mothballed from lack of interest. It's not completely clear which came first, the tourists or UNESCO, but most people will agree on the date: whereas in the early 1990s the town was looking rather forlorn, by 1996 restoration work had begun.

From a traveller's point of view, it's hard to think of a destination with more to offer. Flanked by mountainous limestone cliffs shrouded in mist, Luang Prabang is built on a peninsula defined by the Mekong River on the one side and its tributary the Khan River on the other. The surrounding area is still pristine in its sparsely inhabited agrarian purity, and just outside of town you will come across Lao hill tribes in all their traditional finery. For those with enough time on their hands, the six- to eight-hour journey by car to Vientiane takes you through a slice of Asia most people will never see: a countryside of waterfalls, rice paddies and customs unchanged by the march of modernity. It was by way of such a drive that Ivan Scholte first ended up in Luang Prabang. A British expat who has been living in Asia for almost two decades, he has been, among other

things, a Hong Kong-based wine importer and an organizer of guided antique-hunting expeditions through the backwaters of Southeast Asia. His real ambition was, however, to own and operate a hotel and restaurant, and it was his discovery of Luang Prabang in 2000 that finally cemented his resolve. At the time there were no direct flights, and visitors consisted mainly of Lonely Planet backpackers. There were only two upmarket hotels in town and just one upmarket restaurant (serving French cuisine). Attracted by Luang Prabang's size, sensuality and sophistication, Scholte took over an existing guesthouse and proceeded to transform it into a hotel to match his vision.

The result is the Apsara, named after the heavenly maidens carved into the gallery walls of Cambodia's Angkor Wat in their thousands. The hotel has introduced a simple but street-wise sophistication to the town's accommodation options. Scholte brought interior designer Niki Fairchild in from Bangkok to assist him with the design, and what they've come up with,

most visitors will agree, ranks as the most chic place in town. Both the restaurant and the rooms reflect a refined sense of taste. The restaurant, for instance, features a polished concrete floor, Chinese-style lanterns hung in multicoloured clusters, a pair of sculptural Burmese offering boxes and a handful of specially commissioned Thai paintings. Aside from the fact that it's one of the best places to eat in town, that the rooms all have views of the river below from their colonial terraces and that it's extremely affordable, the best thing about the Apsara is that it is smack bang in the middle of town. All the cafés, temples and shops are within easy walking distance, and if you're up at 6am you can witness Luang Prabang's thousand-odd monks form a snaking, mile-long, saffron-coloured queue as they go about collecting their daily alms. It's one of the few places in Asia, if not the world, where the town in which you're staying is the reason for spending time there. Simply being in Luang Prabang is all the itinerary you need.

---

address The Apsara, Kingkitsarath Street, Ban Wat Sene, Luang Prabang, Laos

t +856 (0)71 212 420 **f** +856 (0)71 254 252 **e** info@theapsara.com

room rates from US$55

satri house

1975 was a terrible year for Southeast Asia. It was the year Pol Pot's deadly Khmer Rouge entered Phnom Penh; the year the US pulled out of Vietnam; and the year the forces of the Communist Lao People's Democratic Republic (LPDR) took over the landlocked Buddhist kingdom of Laos and ousted its royal family.

The land that the French had romantically described as Shangri-la was suddenly in the hands of a suspicious, dogmatic regime. The intelligentsia and the privileged did the smart thing – they left the country. That's how Lamphoune Voravongsa and her brother ended up in France at the ages of 12 and 11. But although they made it out, their parents didn't. Worse still, the government didn't make it easy for those left behind. The authorities didn't trust them. As a result, Lamphoune's parents were assigned LPDR members to live with them as informers, 24 hours a day, 7 days a week – an almost unimaginable living arrangement. Still, they survived, bolstered by the knowledge that their children were thriving in faraway France.

In fact, Lamphoune ended up living the life of a typical Parisienne. Married to a successful lawyer, she had a daughter, a home in Montmartre and a life that was light years away from the suffering back in Laos. Eventually, however, the situation there softened, and the Cold War-era style of Communism gave way to a model not dissimilar to that of China: a state that tolerates and even encourages capitalism as long as the capitalists play by the government's rules. At the same time that Laos was pulling itself together, Lamphoune's idyll began to fall apart. She and her husband divorced and she learnt the lesson that all expats in Paris discover sooner or later – you can live here all your life, but you'll never be a Parisian. The time had come for her to move back to Asia.

Lamphoune settled in the Laotian capital of Vientiane and set up a shop selling jewelry of her own design, as well as Laotian raw silks. It was a success, and because many of her customers were foreigners she saw an opportunity to expand the business to Luang Prabang, a town that was opening itself to tourism in the same way as Siem Reap in Cambodia. Lamphoune's boutiques in Luang Prabang turned out to be so popular that she finally moved there herself.

There were definitely no plans for a hotel until one of her shop managers invited Lamphoune to her home for dinner.

Polished wooden floors, handwoven silks, warm colours and Asian antiques define Satri House's interiors.

Luang Prabang is a sleepy but beautiful UNESCO-listed village situated on the mighty Mekong River.

Satri House's garden and architecture are straight out of the film *Indochine*: lush, tropical and colonial.

Formerly a colonial mansion, Satri House combines late nineteenth-century French refinement with Asian elegance.

Bathrooms are spacious and immaculate, and completely different for each guestroom.

Black-and-white photos, four-poster beds and polished timber floors are common to all bedrooms.

The Frenchwoman was renting a handsome colonial mansion on the outskirts of town, a house of such style and charm that Lamphoune was instantly smitten. Then, as fate would have it, the building's landlord called out of the blue and asked her whether she would be interested in buying it. She was – and she did. And that's how Satri House came into being.

Literally translated, Satri House means house of women. Not only is it owned and operated exclusively by women, which is still quite unusual in Laos, but it is also an environment with a distinctly feminine signature. From the fabrics (raw silk and linen) to the antiques (Chinese, Vietnamese and Thai) to the details such as the china and the art, there is a pervasive sensuousness here that reflects unmistakably a woman's touch. It's the kind of hotel that is wonderfully well suited to a long stay: it is spacious and luxurious with a splendid swimming pool and a completely private garden, but it still

feels like a home. The French may not have been as successful or efficient as the Brits in imperial terms, but they certainly left behind some very lovely architectural souvenirs; French colonial townhouses remain desirable throughout Southeast Asia, and Satri House is a particularly compelling example. With its terracotta-tiled floors, shuttered windows and neoclassical detailing, the building is straight out of the film *Indochine* starring Catherine Deneuve – it could have been used as a location for the film because Satri House is literally overflowing with colonial allure.

Unlike the Apsara, Satri House is not in the middle of town; you don't get the monks but you do get the silence. As a hotel, it's the perfect *yin* to the Apsara's *yang*. They complement each other, which is apt because the proprietors of the Apsara and Satri House are an item. Together, their hotels epitomize the spiritual and aesthetic appeal of Luang Prabang.

address Satri House, 057 Phothisarath Road, Ban That Luang, Luang Prabang, Laos
t +856 (0)71 253 491   **f** +856 (0)71 253 491   **e** info@satrihouse.com
room rates from US$75

the strand

The Eastern & Oriental (E&O) on Penang, Raffles in Singapore and the Strand in Burma (now Myanmar) are the most legendary hotels of the Orient's recent past. They were the life's work of one family – a family that redefined the notion of hospitality in the Far East.

Martin, Tigran, Aviet and Arshak Sarkies were brothers from a long line of Armenian traders who originally made their reputation in the hustle and bustle of Persia's bazaars. Whereas their ancestors profited from trading goods that travelled along the old spice route, the Silk Road immortalized by Marco Polo, this new generation of Sarkies went elsewhere in search of a place to apply their skills in wheeling and dealing. Thus in the latter part of the 1800s the Sarkies brothers moved to the island of Penang where, on a busy street in George Town, they established the E&O, the first in a string of celebrated Asian hotels. Their timing couldn't have been better. One of the most ambitious engineering projects of the Victorian era had recently been completed: the long-awaited, British-built Suez Canal. From the day the first steamers made their way from the Mediterranean to the Red Sea and on to the Indian Ocean, journey time to the Orient had been cut in half, from six weeks to three.

Travel entrepreneurs such as Thomas Cook didn't take long to capitalize on this historic development, and soon elegantly appointed luxury liners were taking the first tourists to the Far East.

By this time, the Sarkies family had fanned out over Asia to repeat the success of Penang's E&O. Their approach was quite systematic: they would first study a location strategically, and once they decided on a site, nothing would be held back in terms of comfort and hospitality. Theirs was a level of luxury previously unheard of in Asia. Whereas earlier hoteliers in the region would have been proud to offer running water, the Sarkies brothers measured themselves by the standards set by such hotels as the Ritz in Paris. Fine porcelain, silverware, crystal chandeliers, monogrammed linen sheets, electric fans, hot and cold running water, caviar, champagne… the latest modern conveniences were combined with the ultimate luxuries. In Singapore they created Raffles, which quickly established itself as one of Asia's most legendary hotels. And in Burma they built the Strand, at a time when the country was one of the most desirable destinations in Asia. The 'road to Mandalay' was a catchphrase for an exotic journey, and

the temple-strewn fields of Pagan were a mandatory stop along the way.

In its heyday, the three-storey, rather imposing stone building with its handsome portico and profusion of stone pillars played host to the likes of Rudyard Kipling, Somerset Maugham, George Orwell, Thomas Cook, the Aga Khan, the odd king, countless titled nobility and more than a handful of international playboys and industrialists. The Strand was *the* place to stay in Burma, and it featured prominently on most itineraries for travellers on a tour of the Far East. But ironically, the hotel's link to the British empire would also be the cause of its ultimate decline. British rule in Burma was never popular, and two successive world wars strengthened the country's resolve to cut all ties with Mother England. Burma's final expulsion of the British by its Communist Party led to independence in 1948, and this super-luxurious colonial-era institution became an awkward reminder of former times.

Nevertheless, despite many sad years of neglect, the Strand always stayed open for business, and there are plenty of hair-raising stories of what it was like to stay here in the years between Burmese independence and the early 1990s. As it happens, one of the storytellers was my father, and judging from his dinner-party anecdotes the place was desperately in need of a lick of paint; simply switching on a light was at the guest's own risk. Another guest in residence when the Strand was not exactly in its prime was Adrian Zecha. People who know Zecha are not in the least surprised that it was he who put up his hand when the Burmese government asked for bids for the renovation of the famous Strand. For Zecha, it was almost a duty to revitalize this former grande dame. Having won the tender, he proceeded to turn it into a worthy reminder of what it once must have been. Today, it's a handy starting point for a journey into a country that hasn't featured on the travel agenda of the Orient for quite some time.

address The Strand, 92 Strand Road, Yangon, Myanmar
t +95 (0)1 243 377   **f** +95 (0)1 243 393   **e** info@thestrand.com.mm
room rates from US$450

dwarika's

It's the hotel of a thousand nooks and crannies. Hidden behind an extraordinary array of intricate wooden screens, spread out among half a dozen irregularly laid-out traditional Nepalese buildings and connected by a series of walkways, bridges and carved pillars, Dwarika's is a place for people who appreciate authenticity with a dash of eccentricity. It's more than a hotel; it's an environment, and it is without question the best place to stay in Kathmandu. Dwarika's cleverly introduces you to Nepalese culture and traditions without sacrificing creature comforts. Staying here, you will learn more about Nepalese food, craft and architecture than you ever would at the Hyatt or the Hilton, or even backpacking around the Himalayas for a couple of months.

It all started, strangely enough, in 1952 when Dwarika Das Shrestha, a Nepali tour operator, was taking his morning exercise in Kathmandu. He was jogging by the ruins of an old building torn down to make way for a modern structure, and came across some workers taking apart an exquisitely carved wooden pillar. They were trying to salvage the wood and regarded the carving as nothing more than a hindrance. On sheer impulse, Shrestha gave the men new timber in exchange for the carved artifact, with no idea of what he would do with it. So began a lifetime quest to preserve Kathmandu's Newari heritage, a once rich artistic legacy of bronze, woodcarving and terracotta in what was not long ago a forgotten medieval Hindu kingdom. Whenever an ancient building was about to be torn down, he would rush in and purchase all the rescuable decorative art, and before long his collection was scattered in makeshift sheds all over his garden. The most logical thing to do with his finds was to construct a building, and he decided to combine tourism and building conservation for the greater good of the Kathmandu Valley by opening a guesthouse. He argued, reasonably, that visitors to Nepal would prefer to stay somewhere authentic – and he was right. Sure enough, the hotel quickly expanded from one small building into the village-like compound it is today.

As Dwarika's developed, so did Shrestha's conservation efforts. No longer satisfied with simply saving historical relics, he set up a school that would train craftsmen in the near-extinct Newari tradition of woodcarving. The same dedication was applied to architecture. Traditional Nepalese terracotta structures are distinguished not just by their unique shape

Bronze details such as this door handle reflect a regard for authentic style not found in any other Nepalese hotel.

Saving traditional Nepalese carved doorways and windows from destruction is how Dwarika's started.

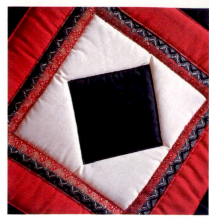

Red, black and white: the colours of the Nepalese flag are used throughout the hotel, from fabrics to staff uniforms.

With spectacular fountains and quiet hidden courtyards, Dwarika's feels more like an enchanted village than a hotel.

Bedrooms are light and spacious; Nepalese decor is limited to fabrics and the odd piece of furniture.

The power of Dwarika's is the way history and tradition are integrated into a cultural experience.

but by their apparently mortarless brickwork; in fact, the bricks are tapered to hide their cement. As these bricks were no longer being manufactured, Shrestha had them made just outside the Kathmandu Valley. At the same time, he developed a manufacturing process that used moulds to mimic woodcarving motifs, thus making it possible to create a traditional building facade at a much lower cost.

If all of this sounds dry and overly technical, the result is anything but. Dwarika's is primarily a place to enjoy Nepal's unique culture (even if construction detail isn't high on your things-to-see list). For example, its restaurant Krishnarpan transports you all over Nepal by serving dishes from various parts of the country. *Momo* (steamed dumplings) are from a region near the Chinese border and hence are reminiscent of dim sum. By contrast, *roti* (unleavened bread) and *palungo ko saag* (sautéed spinach) come from the southeast, near the border with India, and bear a strong similarity to Indian dishes. Everything in the

restaurant is in accordance with Nepalese custom: no shoes on the oiled teak floor, low tables and floor cushions designed for eating cross-legged, and staff dressed in traditional Nepalese clothes that correspond to the regions from which the different dishes originate. It's a sophisticated and engaging way to sample the surprisingly complex and subtle local cuisine.

If you talk to people who are lucky enough to have visited Kathmandu twenty-odd years ago, they will tell you about a tantalizingly exotic medieval Hindu town. Alas, the Kathmandu of today is modernizing at breakneck speed. That said, it's still a very beautiful place, and the surrounding Himalayas, with their rural villages, have changed far less. Many adventurers who arrive in Nepal will confess that they are drawn to the exotic nature of the country more than the trekking, and in that respect Dwarika's has embarked upon exactly the right approach: it allows the guest to soak in the authentic charm of Nepal, without a hint of a blister.

address Dwarika's, P.O. Box 459, Battisputali, Kathmandu, Nepal
t +977 (0)1 447 0770 **f** +977 (0)1 447 1379 **e** info@dwarikas.com
room rates from US$110

cheong fatt tze

He was known as the Rockefeller of the East. When Cheong Fatt Tze arrived in the Straits from Guandong province in China in 1856, he was barely sixteen and penniless. By the time he passed away in 1916 at the age of seventy-six, he had amassed one of the greatest fortunes in the Orient. Such was his stature that on his death, British and Dutch colonial authorities ordered their flags to be flown at half-mast.

Cheong Fatt Tze's ascent from rags to riches began with his first job in Batavia (now Jakarta), the old colonial capital of the Dutch East Indies. He soon came to the notice of his employer, and not only did he rise through the ranks but he ended up marrying the boss's daughter. At the height of his career in the 1890s, he was Consul General for China in Singapore, adviser to the Manchu Dowager Empress Cixi and a director of China's railways and first modern bank. Dubbed 'China's last Mandarin and first capitalist', Cheong's cultural duality was an asset. Completely Oriental in his dress and mannerisms, he could be onvincingly Occidental when he needed to be. First and foremost, though, he was a trader, dealing in the most valued goods of the era, from spices and rubber to the illicit but lucrative commodity of opium.

With great wealth came great spoils. Cheong had eight wives and many more houses, but his favourite residence was the mansion he built on the island of Penang, in the bustling trading port of George Town. It was here that he chose to bring up his sons and spend most of his time. The so-called Blue House (due to its distinctive indigo-painted exterior) was purpose-built to show off his financial prowess. It was flamboyantly extravagant, with thirty-eight rooms, five courtyards, seven staircases and – to counter the heat – two hundred and twenty windows. It also reflected Cheong's multicultural personality. The layout was essentially Chinese, with strict adherence to the discipline of *feng shui*; but the detail was engagingly eclectic, with English Stoke-on-Trent ceramic floor tiles, Scottish cast iron balustrading, French Art Nouveau stained glass windows, Chinese cut-and-paste porcelain, and Gothic louvred teak windows. Not only is it one of the largest Chinese houses ever built outside of China, but it's a formidable example of nineteenth-century Straits Settlement architecture.

Cheong left behind a will dedicated to protecting his legacy, with care taken to ensure that his favourite mansion would be preserved

amanpulo

Poor Philippines: what with modern-day pirates in the south, renegade Communists in the north and Islamic rebels on the Muslim island of Mindanao, what's a traveller to think?

The ironic thing about this quandary is that all these problems exist largely because the Philippines is one of the most democratic nations in Asia. In a region of strict authoritarian governments, the country has become a handy haven for outlaws; it's the downside to democracy, and trouble zones are by no means particular to the Philippines – there are parts of New York City and even London that travellers would be ill-advised to visit. As with anywhere else, the key is knowing what and where they are.

An archipelago of seven thousand-odd islands, many of which are uninhabited, the Philippines is home to a multitude of remote pockets of land separated not just by vast stretches of the Sulu, South China or Philippine Seas, but also by the almost complete absence of infrastructure. In the majority of the country's islands, you are as safe and as blissfully isolated as a tiny pearl in the Caribbean. Perhaps the bigger question, then, is this: out of all the travel choices available in Asia, why go to the Philippines?

The answer lies in both its culture and geography. With its history of Spanish and American colonialism and the Malay-Polynesian roots of its people, this nation is culturally unique. It also has some of the most exquisite tropical islands in the world.

Of all of these, the one that comes closest to perfection is Pamalican, just north of Palawan, an hour's charter flight from Manila. Until 1993, this private island in the Cuyo Group was operated as a family-run coconut plantation. Then, after an extensive makeover, it re-emerged as Amanpulo, Aman's sole property in the Philippines and by all accounts the best and most desirable destination in the entire archipelago. Writers, journalists and magazine editors have trawled their descriptive vocabularies for the right word to pinpoint the brilliant colour of the surrounding Sulu Sea: is it crystal blue, peacock blue or aquamarine? Whatever the precise Pantone shade, the point is that this retreat comes closer to the utopian ideal of a tropical island than any other. The beaches are a brilliant white, the sand is fine and powdery, the water is startlingly clear and the five miles of nearby reefs with their brightly coloured fantasy fish look like a real-life version of Nemo's playground.

The virtues of this paradise are evident; the logistical practicalities are not. Amanpulo is completely self-sufficient: it generates its own power, treats its own sewage, creates its own fresh water from desalination plants and even recycles its own scrap metal. None of this registers with the guests, however, who are blissfully toe-deep in the sand. And why should it? The idea of escape, particularly in a contemporary context, is that someone else makes the decisions for you.

Design-wise, the resort reinforces the sense of beach, with pebble-washed walls and coconut-and-seashell tables. But in true Aman style, it also takes into account the fact that you're in the Philippines. Amanpulo's *casitas* are loosely modelled on the Philippine *bahay kubo* (village home) even though in all honesty, at 450 square feet, they are larger than the average fisherman's hut. Traditionally these houses would have been roofed with coconut palm fronds, but for the sake of pragmatism Aman have used wooden shingles.

Nonetheless, plenty of other details remain true to the local vernacular: for instance, nearly half of the casita is dedicated to a Cebu-marble bathroom, and all the structural timber, including columns and rafters, is made from Philippine *lawan* wood. Even the furniture, from the handwoven rattan chairs from Cebu to the coconut-inlaid tables, reflects both local materials and traditions. And in a brilliantly subtle nod to the nation's colonial heritage, the terraces of the clubhouse are paved in *piedra china* from Manila Bay – the same stone once used as ballast in Chinese ships and Spanish galleons sailing to the Philippines in the 1600s.

Tyrrany, terrorism, the odd typhoon – the Philippines has seen it all in recent times, but there are signs that the nation is about to enter a long period of sustained prosperity and stability. There's plenty of foreign investment, particularly from Hong Kong. Even Imelda Marcos, the one with all the shoes, has been rehabilitated as a well-heeled Congresswoman.

address Amanpulo, Pamalican Island, Philippines

t +63 2 759 4040 **f** +63 2 759 4044 **e** amanpulo@amanresorts.com

room rates from US$625

amanpuri

More than sixteen years after it first opened, this extraordinary complex on Phuket's Sanui Beach is still the most mesmerizing hotel in Thailand. It's not just because of its idyllic location on a private crescent of white sand framed by a verdant amphitheatre of palm tree-clad hills; or its super-chic, all-black horizon pool; or the food, which is easily the best of all the Amans. Amanpuri has something that's difficult to put into words. It has to do with the fact that it's very unusual and yet very Thai, a thoroughly contemporary place with a vernacular aesthetic that doesn't resort to or rely on cliché.

Often design, at least the quality of design, is judged by time. It's not so much about something aging well; it's about not aging at all, which is the category Amanpuri falls in. If anything, it looks better than when it first opened in 1988 because the landscaping has had a chance to mature. Apart from the increased height of the palm trees, the only evidence that years have passed is perhaps the fact that the bathrooms are not as spectacular as those of more recently completed Amans. Over the past decade and a half, bathrooms have been getting larger and sleeker, and while Amanpuri's

bathrooms are by no means small, they are no longer as groundbreaking as they were when the hotel first opened. But surely that's part of Amanpuri's contribution. All the things we now take for granted in luxury accommodation were pioneered by this first Aman: no reception desk, bellboys or lobby; no checking in or out; the idea of a private bungalow; a well-stocked library; and the notion of space, plenty of space, to allow the guest to experience a real escape. All of these are Aman inventions, and Amanpuri was the first. Judging by the present-day state of Phuket, few people have taken a leaf from Aman's book. Phuket property development is in overdrive with very little regard for quality, integrity, cultural consistency or ecology. Not many lessons have been learnt.

Still, despite unattractive prospects by the dozen, Amanpuri preserves the dream of Phuket as an escape destination, largely because it's isolated within its own bay with its own beach. For better or for worse, Phuket, formerly known as Junk Ceylon (a Western corruption of the Malay 'Tanjung Salong' or Cape Salong), has changed beyond recognition. In light of Amanpuri's distinct brand of 'barefoot in the sand' luxury, you could be

Phuket is a seductive blend of waving
palms, white beaches and
turquoise waters.

At Amanpuri, the concept of a bathroom
as large as the bedroom was launched;
now it has become the Asian norm.

At night, Amanpuri's distinctively
Thai architecture has even
more impact.

The beauty of Amanpuri is the convincing way traditional forms have been used without nostalgia.

Guestrooms are the essence of simplicity: white walls, modern lamps, Thai shutters and the odd orchid.

Spectacular landscaping, design and architecture are infused with the cultural signature of Thailand.

forgiven for thinking that Phuket was only a recently discovered beach destination. Yet for centuries the island has been of strategic importance to the rulers of Siam. From early times, Arab traders came Junk Ceylon for its abundance of tin. The mining of tin was considered the exclusive province of the king of Siam, and its extraction, refinement and sale were subject to substantial royal taxation. But despite these hefty levies, tin was a lucrative trade and Junk Ceylon's mines attracted the business of Chinese immigrants. The island's southern port of Bukit became the main hub for the shipping of the much-coveted metal. Thus, a remote part of Siam came to the simultaneous attention of the Thai royal family, Arab traders, Indian merchants and seafaring European entrepreneurs. Within Asia, the island has been swapped back and forth several times between the mighty Khmer empire of Cambodia based in Angkor and the Mon empire based at Sukhothai, later known as the kingdom of Siam. The only thing that hasn't

changed is the descriptions of the island's beauty. From French sea captains to British journalists and even Swedish scientists, there are numerous records that testify to the island's natural endowment, and almost without exception, each and every writer refers to its exquisite beaches framed by the dense green of rainforest immediately beyond. There's even a specific reference to the Bay of Patong, though no one who knew it then would recognize this current victim of overdevelopment. As it turns out, the beauty of Junk Ceylon has ultimately become more exportable than tin. Blessed with a climate conducive to beach life year-round, Phuket, as the island eventually came to be known, has developed into one of the most famous resort destinations in the world.

The appeal of Amanpuri is best summed up by a guest. 'I haven't been to any other Amans,' he volunteered. 'Why should I? I can't imagine it would be better than here – how could it be? Every time I leave the property, even for a few hours, I always end up regretting it.'

address Amanpuri, Pansea Beach, Phuket 83000, Thailand

t +66 (0)76 324 333 **f** +66 (0)76 324 100 **e** amanpuri@amanresorts.com

room rates from US$675

la flora

Phuket is without a doubt one of the most recognized and desired destinations in Asia. It conjures visions of tropical beaches, virgin forests of swaying palms and turquoise blue waters. Add to this the appeal of Thai cuisine and the beauty of the Thai people and you have all the ingredients for an escape to paradise. As with many beach destinations, however, expectations can often surpass reality. Yes, there are perfect beaches and lots of palm trees in Phuket, but there are also four-lane highways and alarmingly wayward property development − a case of too many shops, too many hotels, and definitely too many Irish pubs.

The truth is that the ideal of Phuket is only to be found in singular examples and locations; in the odd oasis of style and natural beauty amidst the chaos of overheated property development. No wonder then that the trend lately has been to spread out: getting further away from the airport is the answer to finding (and keeping) a slice of Andaman Sea beach that's still like the brochures. That's how La Flora ended up almost forty miles north of Phuket airport. In fact, it's not even on the island of Phuket at all; it's on the western coast of mainland Thailand, just north of

Phuket itself. But this is a technicality. Access to La Flora is still via Phuket International Airport. And more to the point it offers what people want from Phuket: palm trees, empty unspoilt beaches, turquoise waters, blue skies, tropical heat and elegant luxury.

Long-term, La Flora's location is safe from out-of-control developers because it's surrounded by national park. Architecturally there's a nod to a Thai vernacular. Arranged directly along the beach, La Flora's guest villas are essentially open-plan bungalows with Japanese-style platform beds and indoor as well as outdoor bathrooms. In the context of Asian accommodation, they are what we have come to expect of an upmarket resort. But the villas at La Flora come with two unexpected twists: first, they're surprisingly affordable, and second, they are distinctly stylized. They're not so much minimal as modern, featuring a *Wallpaper** magazine approach to a beach resort: funky in that bad-taste, disco-dancing sort of way. The interiors are decorated with the kind of metallic-coloured, abstract floral feature walls that were a big hit in the sixties. If it were not combined with dark wooden furniture, an open-plan arrangement and lofty ceiling height, I'm not sure it would work.

But it does, and it distinguishes La Flora's guest villas from all the other ones around. It also makes sense of the name, even though I suspect it was meant to refer more to the verdant setting of a national park than the retro detailing of the rooms.

One thing is certain: La Flora provides the kind of isolation that many travellers look for when heading to the tropical beaches of Southeast Asia. You often have the beach to yourself because there is only one other hotel on this very long stretch of sand. But being so isolated has its downside: there are no towns, no bars and no other restaurants. La Flora is thus decidedly not for singles, which in itself reflects another fast-emerging trend in Asia: the isolated escape hotel intended for couples that don't plan on leaving their rooms very much. It's the honeymoon market, which by all accounts is big business in Asia. La Flora has only just opened and it does the honeymoon thing very well – too well, at times. Shortly after my arrival, I was just settling into my room when I heard a knock at the door. I could see that there was someone outside holding a very large tray – a welcome gesture and, by the looks of it, an extravagant one. But rather a strange one. In the past I've had baskets of fruit, bowls of fruit, dried fruit, chocolate-covered fruit, chocolate, large bottles of champagne, tiny bottles of champagne…but I've never, ever had a chocolate cake, and certainly not a big, round one covered in pink icing sugar roses with a card that reads 'Happy Anniversary'. Sometimes things get lost in translation, but this clearly was not my cake. I did my best to explain that I was alone and it takes two to celebrate an anniversary, but his response was the same each time: 'No, 502 for you.' It's true that I was staying in bungalow 502, but although my refusal to take the cake was making him sad, I had no choice but to push him and his chocolate cake back to the reception. It's a tale that highlights the extraordinary level of hospitality throughout Asia, and funky La Flora is no exception.

address La Flora, 59/1 Moo 5 Tambon Khuk-Khak, Takuapa Phang-Nga 82190, Thailand

t +66 (0)76 428 000 **f** +66 (0)76 428 029 **e** laflora@sanctuaryresorts.com

room rates from Baht 3,900

w seoul-walkerhill

This is Asia's first W and probably the most cutting-edge, funky, no-holds-barred, leave-no-design-stone-unturned W in the world. With three restaurants, an immense lounge built as a series of ascending staircases, a very serious gym, an even more serious spa and a completely over-the-top swimming pool, this is the biggest event in Seoul and the only place like it South Korea. So why did W, the Starwood group's 'couture' hotel chain, choose Seoul as their entry into Asia? Because Seoul is Asia's Seattle.

South Korea used to be one of the most traditional countries in Asia. But now, on the back of its economic success, this nation's northern capital spread along the Han River is hip, shiny and new, fuelling a homegrown creativity that has fans as far away as Indonesia. Seoul's brand new airport, for instance, is a futuristic, gleaming, bug-shaped fantasy that makes other airports, including Hong Kong and Osaka, look conservative by comparison. Attention to detail and spotless cleanliness seem to be a distinctly Korean attribute. It's the only airport I've been to where you're given slippers to wear while your shoes are going through X-ray, and where the men's room displays the janitor's name, photograph

and his cleaning licence so you know whose fault it is if it isn't spotless.

Framed by local mountain peaks (skiing is only an hour's drive away), straddling the broad river on both sides, Seoul is handsomely situated. Architecturally, it's typical of new cities: clusters of glass-clad, high-rise towers punctuating random, low-rise density. But as a metropolis, the city is quite attractive, particularly at night when all the bridges are illuminated with a distinctive cobalt blue light. The W's location in Seoul is one of its most potent attractions, and this is by no means an accident – it's fundamental to the group's philosophy. The point is that the three restaurants – the Kitchen, Namu and Tonic – and the WooBar, the longest bar in Korea, are not just meant for hotel guests. If they were, they could be ten times smaller. They were designed to attract the locals. Why? Because the W sets out to create a 'scene', a venue for young urbanites to hang out for after-work drinks, dinner and the rest. And that means the overnight guest from out of town enjoys the added plus of staying in a place that's a hot destination in its own right. Normally the choices that face the short-term traveller (almost everyone these days) are not promising

in a new city. You can either play it safe by staying in to watch a movie and order room service, or you can put your life in the hands of a concierge and taxi driver and hope that their idea of a good time is the same as yours. Not too many people opt for choice number two – a case of better safe than sorry. But if you stay in a place that's hot, you can impress your local contacts with your hipness, because going out is simply a matter of stepping into the elevator. The argument is simple: if the hotel you're staying in *is* the scene then you have no incentive to leave the premises – you can be a guilt-free stick-in-the-mud.

Achieving such a scene, however, is no mean task. In the case of this W, it required enormous investment. It's all very well to be the most innovative hotel in South Korea's capital, but the restaurants still have to deliver the goods and the staff still have to provide the service. What's more, even the most modern-minded among us can be predictably conservative when it comes to spending money. Despite its size – with over 250 rooms – the hotel manages to deliver on all fronts. The Kitchen, an Italian–Mediterranean restaurant with an Asian twist, does fusion cuisine very well, while Namu, the Oriental alternative, is a sophisticated combination of sushi bar, teppanyaki grill and private dining rooms. But that's not all. The forest of neon poles that defines the entry space, the white and red media rooms with their round beds and round red bathtubs, the spa guestrooms with their mini-swimming pools bang by the window, the elevators with their illuminated gymnastics rings hanging from the ceiling…all of this is meant to impress, and it does – no one more than the Koreans themselves. Whether they enter in groups or in individual dribs and drabs, the effect seems to be the same. None of them have seen anything like it before, and that's exactly what the W Seoul is banking on. Did I mention the red Jags with the white interiors that they send to pick you up at the airport?

address W Seoul-Walkerhill, 21 Gwangjang dong, Gwangjin- gu, Seoul 143 708, Korea
t +82 (0)2 465 2222 **f** +82 (0)2 450 4989 **e** wseoul@whotels.com
room rates from Won 435,000

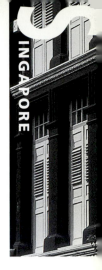

1929

Cut your hair or get out. That was the rule in Singapore. No long hair (on men), no hippies. For years after Singapore separated from Malaysia in 1965, its stern founding father Lee Kuan Yew had little time for subversive elements – he was too busy building a nation. In the meantime, barber chairs awaited offending visitors at Singapore's international airport, and anyone who rejected 'short back and sides' was turned away on the spot.

But give credit where it's due: it's hard to think of another country that has grown so much in so short a time. The Singapore we know today was created in the space of two decades. The city was at once sanitized and modernized. Littering, chewing gum and spitting in the street became unlawful offences, while most of the city's colonial architecture disappeared. Out went the elegant stucco 'shophouses' of Chinatown (so named because of the shops downstairs and shopkeepers' residences upstairs); in came the steel and glass towers and American-style shopping malls.

It's conceivable that every last shophouse would have been pulled down if the newly prosperous Singaporeans hadn't taken a last-minute interest in their country's cultural and architectural heritage. Fortunately in the

mid-1980s these distinctive shuttered buildings became the subject of a determined conservation drive. And just in time, too. Only a few of Chinatown's shophouse-lined streets such as Keong Saik Road were saved from developers' demolition balls. Now they host some of the city's hottest bars, clubs and restaurants – not to mention the red-light district. If it comes as a revelation that Singapore even has a red-light district, it should be less surprising that it's one of the few places in the city where there's a street scene. People sit on outdoor terraces eating noodles, drinking beer and smoking, amidst karaoke bars and groovy little restaurants that are Parisian in size and New York in style.

In the heart of all this lies Hotel 1929. Made up of five shophouses built in 1929 (hence the name), this is not the first hotel to spring up in Chinatown, but it's certainly the first to abandon the predictable mahogany and brass furnishings of colonial interiors. Outside, the building has been kept exactly as it was, winning it a conservation award. Inside, any restraint or traditionalism has been abandoned with gusto. Proprietor Loh Lik Peng has a passion for twentieth-century designer chairs, and his collection sets the tone of the hotel.

This is a place for people who know the difference between Marimekko and Mies van der Rohe; for design cognoscenti who can spot a Verner Panton 'Cone' chair or an Arne Jacobsen 'Egg' chair from a mile away. And in case you have any doubts, there's a large poster hanging in the lift that illustrates the chair collection from the Vitra Design Museum – many of which are in 1929. That said, it's not just the furniture that distinguishes the hotel. The architecture stands out too: thirty-two rooms and not a single square angle. But what makes the place really unique is its location. The reaction of taxi drivers when you give them the address only adds to the fun. And this is the keyword: 1929 is the first hotel I would call fun in Singapore.

Yet there's more to 1929's surrounding area than a bit of local sexiness. It also happens to be a hub for trendy cuisine. Like New York, Singapore has plenty of young restaurant-hunters, and one of their favourite stalking grounds is Chinatown. Guests at 1929 don't have far to go to experience some of the best dining in town. In fact, the restaurant, Ember, is just an elevator-ride away from your room, and it's currently one of *the* places to be seen in Singapore. The Scandinavian-inspired decor provides a suitably minimalist backdrop for the food, which is cosmopolitan with an Asian signature: don't miss the soft-shell crab with lime and wasabi mayonnaise.

When it's all said and done, there are two choices for accommodation in Singapore. There's the big beige, black and gold hotel that will smother you with corporate hospitality, invariably located near the central business district and Orchard Road, where you'll find the same designer labels you find in every other city. And then there's the 1929 option, a chance to experience the new, vibrant subculture of Singapore, hidden within the few streets that remain from its colonial past. If the decision is still not a no-brainer, consider that a night at 1929 costs the equivalent of a minibar bill elsewhere.

address Hotel 1929, 50 Keong Saik Road, 089154 Singapore

t +65 6347 1929 **f** +65 6327 1929 **e** reservations@hotel1929.com

room rates from S$100

Collection of John Rendell Courtesy of National Archives Singapore

1929

doornberg

Doornberg, or Dutch House as it is also known, used to be the residence of an admiral of the Galle-based Dutch East India Company's merchant navy. Built in 1712, the mansion is a relic of Holland's Golden Age, when trade with the East produced unheard-of riches: at its zenith, the Company counted more than three thousand ships in its fleet, and just one of these laden with spices could generate enough profit for a middle-class *burger* to retire for life.

The key word was trade, and the Dutch were masters at it. The secret was knowing what to trade. The Dutch coveted the spices grown by the people of Java and Sumatra, but what could they offer in return? The traditional European currencies of silver, gold or even linen or velvet were of no interest to the Indonesians, but the *ikat* textiles of India were. Thus the Dutch ships rounding the Cape of Good Hope would head for the Indian region of Hyderabad, load as much ikat as they could carry and then journey down India's coast towards the southern tip of Sri Lanka to the Dutch colonial stronghold of Galle. From there, after a brief stop to reload supplies and rest the crew, they would continue to Batavia (now Jakarta). Full to the brim with spices, they would once again sail to Galle. Unlike

most colonial powers, it was never Holland's intention to colonize Sri Lanka; its aim was just to capitalize on the strategic position of one of its ports. Thus the Dutch invested major time and money into boosting the city's defences.

The remains of Holland's fort-buildings are still to be found in Galle, one of which is Doornberg. Set high on a hillside with an idyllic view of the Bay of Galle, the admiral's former house is a particularly attractive example of Dutch colonial architecture in the tropics: a combination of pared-down, neoclassical columns supporting a series of overhanging verandas with lofty ceilings, long elegant spaces and stately period furniture. The effect, contrary perhaps to what one might expect, is at once terribly grand and surprisingly comfortable – almost cosy. Aside from Doornberg's architectural pedigree and second-to-none location, the added plus here is the fact that the building has survived as a house. Various rooms and spaces are use much as they would have been originally, and the guest at Doornberg experiences something not dissimilar to staying with the admiral himself. All too often, the temptation with hotels is to use existing structures – in this case the main house – as a reception–lobby–office, meaning

Long, tall and spacious – Doornberg's elegant guestrooms are generous in size and colonial in shape.

A pair of wooden clogs in the entrance hall is a gentle reminder of the building's Dutch colonial legacy.

More like an apartment than a hotel room, Doornberg's guest suites feature both a living room and bedroom.

Details such as frangipani flowers in earthenware bowls are casually placed around the property.

Bathrooms are exquisite – probably some of the most refined and spacious in all of Sri Lanka.

Doornberg was once the residence of an admiral of the Dutch East India Company; the car is a new addition.

bedrooms have to be built elsewhere. At Doornberg, there is no lobby or office, and in fact all discernible traces of its function as a hotel have been removed.

This suits Hong-Kong-based English proprietor Geoffrey Dobbs very well indeed. Dobbs's approach to hotels and tourism is to keep things small and sophisticated; his other Galle property, Sun House, has made quite a name worldwide, even though it only has seven rooms. It too is a historic colonial house, but that's where the similarity ends. Where Sun House is fresh, bright and affordable, Doornberg is darker, more chic and somewhat less affordable – you might even say expensive, but it's well worth every penny. The refined furniture and fabrics create the ambience of stately colonial grandeur without the clichés. And not only is each of the staterooms immense, but so are the bathrooms. Doornberg also has beautiful gardens, just as you would expect of a house that once belonged to an admiral. What with the recent addition of an infinity pool discreetly tucked away on one side of the estate, it's easy to forget that the place you're staying in is actually a hotel.

It's difficult to describe the unique atmosphere of this place, but I vaguely recognize it: it reminded me of being at my grandmother's townhouse in the Hague. Doornberg's clever combination of formality and informality, of precious antiques combined with simple rattan, sets it apart in terms of interior design and charm. There's simply nothing else like it in the Orient, and that in itself is reason enough to stay here. But Doornberg's real drawcard is the seductive pace of the place. Doing nothing, very slowly, is the order of the day. No one here seems to be a slave to itineraries, nor is there a continual gathering of people about to depart on sightseeing trips. At Doornberg, you're left with the impression that all the guests have been here for so long that they have completely adjusted to the Sri Lankan way of life – even if they only arrived yesterday.

address Doornberg, c/o Sun House, 18 Upper Dickson Road, Galle, Sri Lanka

t +94 (0)91 4380275   **f** +94 (0)91 2222624   **e** sunhouse@sri.lanka.net

room rates from US$330

taru villas

A completely private getaway by the sea, on a beach with perfect weather…it's an archetypal dream destination. If it also happens to be inspiringly stylish and blessed with great service, it becomes somewhere you're tempted *not* to tell your friends about.

Taru Villas is exactly that. Located just outside the town of Bentota and a three-hour drive from Colombo's international airport, it's the kind of place you can imagine staying for long enough to write a book. Apart from the very tangible benefit of being affordable, Taru's convincing combination of style, sand and service make it worth the flight to Sri Lanka.

Years ago, the pleasures of this tropical island – a milder, gentler, less frenetic version of India – were compromised by the threat of terrorism and violence associated with the independence campaign of the northern Tamil-speaking minority. Now there's a truce. Hostilities between the Hindu Tamils and the Buddhist Sinhalese are confined to the negotiating table, and Sri Lanka's economy is free to get back to marketing the country's remarkable coastline.

Taru Villas was discovered not by visiting sunseekers but by a cosmopolitan crowd from Colombo. Nayantara Fonseka (better known as Taru) is a flamboyant creative figure in the Sri Lankan fashion world, who by the strength of her personality has become synonymous with her own clothes label. For years, she and a few carloads of friends would make the two-and-a-half-hour trek from the city on a Friday evening to spend a relaxed, idyllic weekend on the coast. This became such a fixture in Taru's life that she pledged to take any opportunity she could to pursue her passion for the property and its location. One day it went up for lease – and that's how Taru got into the hotel business.

The place had good bones. Even though the site itself was awkwardly long and narrow, the original architect had been clever with the use of space, and the buildings were arranged to avoid giving the impression of being in a tunnel. The villas, set along a single wall, are subtly oriented so that all of them face different directions. This ensures total privacy, and for guests it's like having your own house.

To this already successful establishment, Taru has brought her sense of style and hospitality. Taru Villas now has the colour, warmth and character that is so often lacking from an architect's disciplined vision. Walls painted a musty shade of pink are juxtaposed with plenty of white, and bright saffron yellow

is combined with black and white (a traditional colonial Portuguese combination). More than anything, though, Taru Villas is a triumph of simplicity. It's not easy to make a place look good with very little, but that's exactly what Taru has done to distinguish this little bolthole on the beach. It's a blend of good choice of colour, interesting selection of furniture and the omnipresent avoidance of clutter.

One of Taru Villas' most unconventional attractions is the train that runs straight through the property. It may not sound like the most desirable feature in a hotel, but it's not as obtrusive as you'd think: the last train stops well before bedtime, and during the day the noise is a gentle reminder of a different age. You have to cross the single railway track to get to the beach – 'cross' not in the sense of pedestrian crossing, but actually stepping over rails and sleepers – and most guests find this both quirky and fun. Running all the way along the coast, the train from Colombo to

Galle claims the best view and location here – something the Sri Lankans may have picked up from the British, whose train routes are also often spectacular.

What surprised me more than the train was the beach. Having been many times to Kerala – the very south of India – as well as the nearby Maldives, I was expecting to find small stretches of sand and calm waters in Bentota. Instead, the beach here reminded me more of Australia than Asia. At Taru Villas it goes on for miles, and the water is wild and woolly enough for some decent bodysurfing. While the current is not dangerous – certainly not by Australian standards – most locals refrain from going in. But visitors shouldn't be deterred. Compared with Bondi the water's usually tame, and the hotel can even lend you a boogie-board.

At Taru Villas you can escape to one of Sri Lanka's best beaches. And at this price you can go barefoot in the sand for as long as you like. Before you know it, you'll be signing your postcards 'Bentota Beach Bum'.

address Taru Villas, 146/4 Galle Road, Robolgoda, Bentota, Sri Lanka

t +94 (0)34 2275618 **f** +94 (0)11 4724632 **e** taprobana@taruvillas.com

room rates from US$91

the lalu at sun moon lake

Sun Moon Lake is an escape destination for the hip, urban residents of Taipei. Taiwan's capital is one of the most vibrant cities in Asia, with great restaurants and an even better nightlife. And that explains what a hotel of the calibre of the Lalu is doing on a lake in Taiwan – even the most metropolitan alleycat needs to get away from it all.

One celebrated Taipei resident who used to make his way to Sun Moon Lake at every opportunity was Chiang Kai-shek, the founder of modern Taiwan and President of the Republic from 1949 to 1975. The hotel features two permanent reminders of this: first, the presidential yacht is still moored on Lalu's pontoon, and second, there's a Chiang Kai-shek Museum right by the entrance. The reference to Taiwan's revered leader is more than just a passing coincidence: the Lalu occupies the site of his former summer residence.

Sun Moon Lake is the largest freshwater lake in Taiwan, covering an area of almost two thousand acres and stretching to over twenty miles in perimeter. Its northern half is shaped like the sun while the southern half resembles a crescent moon, hence the lake's name. The surrounding area was originally inhabited by the Shao, a tribe that practised ancestor worship and believed the lake's island of Lalu to be the holy land of their forebears. Though a once dominant population, their numbers have since declined and today most surviving Shao live in Sun Moon Lake Village, where they are as much of a tourist attraction as the lake itself.

Curiously, the development of tourism in Sun Moon Lake was only made possible by the Japanese, who were the ruling power in Taiwan for over half a century after the Sino-Japanese War in 1895. In 1925 they brought over tea saplings from the Indian state of Assam and set up the Taiwan Tea Experimentation Station at Sun Moon Lake's Mount Mao-lan. Because of the area's altitude, warmth and significant rainfall (similar in many ways to Assam), it developed into one of the world's foremost suppliers of Assam tea. Nowadays each tea plantation produces some three thousand pounds of tea from a single acre (which is apparently a lot). After their success growing tea in the area, the Japanese turned their attention to civil engineering. The upper stream of the Choshui River was diverted into Sun Moon Lake in order to accommodate a power station, which increased the lake's size by a considerable measure. But before the Japanese could start building, they first needed to create roads and railways to reach the area. Thus, access to Sun Moon Lake was first made possible by the infrastructure that the Japanese left behind. Tourists soon followed, who were drawn to the area by the compelling scenery.

Surrounded by mountain ranges situated on the cusp of the lake's reflective basin, the Lalu itself is very much part of the setting. It was certainly a good move to invite Singapore-based architect Kerry Hill to design a structure on such a site. Conceived as an all-suite hotel, the Lalu's ninety-eight rooms, nine villas, three restaurants, two bars and teahouse were designed with two objectives in mind: one, to maximize the view; and two, to cater to every possible anticipated wish of each guest – a seductive combination of extraordinary location and comfort enhanced by the architecture and design. It all sounds fairly straightforward, but it was no easy task to ensure that each suite had a view of the lake and that the hotel retained a sense of its own vernacular, i.e. remaining true to Taiwan's

history yet uncompromisingly modern. But in Hill, the developers had an architect with plenty of experience of blending the traditional with the contemporary in a sexy package: he did it for Amandari in Ubud and more recently for Amansara in Cambodia, not to mention countless houses for private clients throughout Asia. To create the view, Hill designed a single long box running parallel to the edge of the lake. Cleverly, to highlight the intent of the design, the horizontal spread of the building is purposefully magnified by the positioning of an Olympic-sized swimming pool between the lake and the hotel – it makes a feature of the length of the building, which might otherwise read as overly large.

Stylistically, it's difficult to put the Lalu's interiors in a box. They are neither distinctly Chinese nor Japanese. Instead, they represent a sophisticated Asian international aesthetic with both Chinese and Japanese touches – which somehow sums up both the hotel and the nation that hosts it quite well.

address The Lalu, Sun Moon Lake, 142 Jungshing Road, Yuchr Shiang, Nantou 555, Taiwan (R. O. C)

t +886 (0)49 285 5311 **f** 886 (0)49 285 5312 **e** lalu@ghmhotels.com

room rates from NT$13,800

ana mandara

One of the most memorable scenes in Francis Ford Coppola's *Apocalypse Now* is when a succession of army helicopters loaded with surfboards swoops down along the Vietnamese coast in search of some good waves with Wagner's 'Flight of the Valkyrie' blasting at full volume. It is a brief cinematic reminder that Vietnam is not all rice fields, low-lying deltas and mountains dense with tropical jungle. It also has a coastline. In fact, not many countries in Southeast Asia can boast over two thousand miles of continuous coastline as dramatically beautiful as that of Vietnam. From the plane you see crescent after crescent of completely virgin beach with not a single building, village or fishing fleet in sight.

Vietnam's coast is the country's as yet undiscovered pearl. And the government, much to its credit, is not rushing things. Compared to Thailand, the Philippines or Malaysia, Vietnam is virtually undeveloped. Whereas Thailand, for instance, has Phuket, Koh Samui, Hua Hin, Pattaya and Krabi, to name a few well-known beach resorts, Vietnam so far has only one of international standing: Nha Trang. Situated between Hanoi and Ho Chi Minh City on Highway 1, Nha Trang has been the country's main beach destination for many decades.

Even during the Vietnam War, both sides, North and South, would holiday here, conveniently designating it a 'non-aggression zone'.

The area certainly looks promising when you land at the airport. The runway is only a few hundred yards from a stunning stretch of totally deserted beach, flanked by tall, cascading dunes. And the drive to Nha Trang twenty miles away gives you many more glimpses of pristine shore. By contrast, the beach in Nha Trang is certainly not deserted, but neither is it spoilt. A five-mile-long expanse of immaculate sand, it puts the likes of Miami to shame. There's also no high-rise construction by the water. In fact, the only hotel currently on the sand is Ana Mandara, justifiably billed right now as the best hotel in Vietnam. Yet even from the road running along the beach, you'd never even know it was there because its colonial Franco-Viet-style villas disappear among the foliage of the densely planted palm trees.

The clever thing about Ana Mandara is the way it's been built: spread along nearly a mile of beach and nestled in the surrounding greenery, it gives the impression of being a lot smaller than it really is. Even when it's completely full (which is most of the time),

Dining rooms at opposite ends of the beach contribute to the impression that Ana Mandara is never too crowded.

Lily ponds, goldfish, colonial architecture – the hotel is a wealth of collective details.

The Six Senses spa is second to none in Vietnam. The view is of the lotus garden from one of the relaxation cabanas.

Ana Mandara is the only property
in Nha Trang that is actually
on the beach.

Vietnam is still not entirely comfortable
with tourism, and that's part of
its appeal.

The guest bungalows feature polished
wooden floors, lofty ceiling height and
Chinese-inspired furniture.

you'd never know it. Guests are spread out over the fifty-odd-acre complex, where they can choose between two restaurants, a renowned spa, several bars and two different swimming pools, not to mention the beach.

Design-wise, much effort has gone into giving the place a distinct Vietnamese signature: a blend of Chinese motifs, French colonial detailing and Vietnamese artisanal tradition. Female staff wear the *ao dai*, which is probably the most elegant national costume in Asia: a long, tight-fitting tunic split along the sides, worn over silk trousers. They also don a *doac*, a conical reed hat, not so much as a decorative gesture but more because the sun in this region is particularly intense – sun-baking between 11am and 2pm is definitely not a good idea. Visitors need only observe the locals, who cover up completely during the hottest hours of the day: women wear hats and scarves over their faces and long gloves that cover their arms.

A key attraction for coming here is value for money; Vietnam is among the least expensive countries in Asia. Nha Trang is a surprisingly big town, with more than 300,000 inhabitants, which means that if you're prepared to venture from the perfectly groomed confines of Ana Mandara, there's a lot to see and do. The chef, for instance, takes guests along for his morning shopping at local markets at 5am. Or you can visit rice fields where the ritual of the harvest has been unchanged for centuries.

The other attraction of Ana Mandara, of course, is the fact that it is in Vietnam, and the Vietnamese themselves make up a large part of the equation. Although Nha Trang welcomes tourists, the people retain many of their traditions, and as a visitor you have the distinct impression that this is a country that has not given itself over entirely to tourism. Vietnam is unspoilt because the people are unspoilt. They are not jaded about the arrival of foreign visitors, but nor are they slavishly dedicated to them. It's a combination that makes the traveller still feel like a traveller.

---

address Ana Mandara Resort, Beachside Tran Phu Blvd, Nha Trang, Vietnam

t +84 (0)58 829 829 **f** +84 (0)58 829 629 **e** resvana@dng.vnn.vn

room rates from US$185

evason hideaway

It's the perfect name. Situated on a hidden beach on a lush, mountainous peninsula overlooking a series of overlapping bays, the Evason Hideaway is exactly that – you would never even know it's there. From a distance, the enclave of thatched huts on the beach and wooden houses suspended on the rocks is completely invisible. And even as you approach it by boat – the only way to get there – you still need binoculars to pick out the houses nestling in the dense foliage just behind the pristine sands.

With fifty-four individual villas, a spa complex and two restaurants, the Hideaway is clearly more than a few rudimentary beach huts. Yet that's exactly the impression it creates. It's the kind of destination that immediately makes you wonder how it was found in the first place. For many years, this was a secret picnic spot for guests of Ana Mandara. Sheltered from prevailing winds and tucked away from all traces of civilization, it's the ultimate beach fantasy. The possibility of building a retreat in such a place must have occurred to proprietors Eva and Sonu Shivdasani (hence Evason) many times, but it didn't come into being until General Ha Van Dung (pronounced Zoong) entered the picture. A war hero from the

North, the general is also a civil engineer who is now mainly busy with public works for the Socialist Republic of Vietnam in the South: he built Nha Trang's new airport as well as the brand new four-lane concrete highway that leads to it, both to commemorate the late Ho Chi Minh's birthday. Without General Dung, the Hideaway would still be a dream because the land is leased from the military. What's more, the logistical challenge of building on what is essentially an inaccessible site (with no roads whatsoever) falls more within a description of a military exercise than a building project. The military analogy goes even further than one might imagine. Despite the laid-back, Robinson Crusoe ambience of the place, it has taken an army of workers to bring the fantasy to life. More than six hundred labourers have toiled here for almost two years to bring power, sewerage, running water and telecommunications to a completely virgin piece of jungle on the coast. Everything – from the trucks and machinery to the pipes and cables – was brought in by boat, D-Day style. The general and his 'troops' considered building a jetty, but in order to preserve the integrity of the crystalline bay ultimately decided against it. Likewise, everything about

the design – the architecture, the building materials, the manner of construction using interlocking wood with no nails or glue – was chosen with the aim of creating the ultimate escape. The result is a series of huts and houses that represent a new style of luxury: more rugged, raw and natural, with space and privacy as primary considerations.

I've not come across an environment that delivers these ingredients more convincingly than the Hideaway's water villas. Built into and onto the massive boulders scattered along the shore, they are the three-dimensional realization of the ultimate barefoot beach shack. Architecturally they are particularly clever because they are at once completely open and completely private. Constructed entirely in timber – wooden beams, wooden floors, wood-panelled floors, even wooden baths – they are exposed to the elements in every direction, with huge doors that slide back and lead to surrounding decks and verandas, which in turn offer sweeping views of the crescent-shaped beach. But privacy is ensured by the giant rocks that form an integral part of each villa's construction. The boulders are both sculpture and screen, an organic feature and focal point but also a means of naturally separating one villa from the next. Like gigantic organic ornaments, they simultaneously dominate and decorate the cutout views created by the hand-assembled, interlocking timber architecture.

The sublime irony of this extraordinary place is that General Dung himself has little idea how special it is because he has nothing to compare it to. As part of a peculiar hangover from the previously embattled Socialist regime, he is unable to travel overseas; the government refuses to give him a passport, ostensibly because as a war hero he holds many state secrets. Thus Dung has never had a chance to visit other countries or indeed resorts, so he's probably not aware that staying here is an experience akin to residing in an Isamu Noguchi art installation.

---

address Evason Hideaway at Ana Mandara, Beachside Tran Phu Blvd, Nha Trang, Vietnam

t +84 (0)58 829 829   **f** +84 (0)58 829 629   **e** resvana@dng.vnn.vn

room rates from US$400

First published in the United Kingdom in 2005 by Thames & Hudson Ltd, 181A High Holborn, London WC1V 7QX

www.thamesandhudson.com

British Library Cataloguing-in-Publication Data
A catalogue record for this book is available from the British Library

ISBN-13: 978-0-500-28513-8
ISBN-10: 0-500-28513-6

Printed and bound in Singapore by CS Graphics

Acknowledgments
Photography by Herbert Ypma, with the exception of Amankora, Amanpulo, the Lalu at Sun Moon Lake, Sila Six Senses (p.156 and p.161) and Uma Paro, supplied courtesy of the hotels.

Designed by Maggi Smith